# MumLife

## LOUISE PENTLAND

### WHAT NOBODY EVER TELLS YOU ABOUT BEING A MUM

First published in the UK by Blink Publishing
An imprint of Bonnier Books UK
Wimpole Street, London, W1G 9RE
Owned by Bonnier Books
Sveavägen 56, Stockholm, Sweden

www.blinkpublishing.co.uk

facebook.com/blinkpublishing
twitter.com/blinkpublishing

Hardback – 978-1-788-702-92-8
eBook – 978-1-788-702-93-5
Audiobook – 978-1-788-703-05-5
Paperback – 978-1-788-704-13-7



A CIP catalogue of this book is available from the British Library.

Typeset by IDSUK (Data Connection) Ltd
Printed and bound in Great Britain by Clays Ltd, Elcograf S.p.A.

1 3 5 7 9 10 8 6 4 2


First published in 2020 by Blink Publishing
This edition first published in 2021 by Blink Publishing
Illustrations and chapter titles designed by © Emily Courdelle

*For each book sold Bonnier Books UK shall donate 1% of net receipts and Louise Pentland shall donate 100% of her royalties to the NSPCC.*

## LOUISE PENTLAND

is the *Sunday Times* bestselling author of the Wilde novels trilogy. She's the number one parenting vlogger in the UK, with 8 million combined followers across her social platforms. Louise is the creator and host of the podcast Mothers' Meeting, where she interviews fellow mums and discusses all things motherhood.

Louise featured on the 2019 '*Sunday Times* Top 100 Influencers' list and was crowned as the number one 'mumfluencer' of 2019 by *Mother & Baby*. She was also a UN Global Ambassador for Gender Equality. Louise has filmed with an array of people, from Kim Kardashian to the Pope at the Vatican. She is also involved in the support and encouragement of

Bookstart, alo

the Du

Praise for

# Mumlife

'An honest account of becoming a woman and mother . . . an engaging read'

GIOVANNA FLETCHER

'Hilarious, honest, heartwarming, like a hug from a friend, just perfect. I couldn't love this "mumoir" more – Louise has managed to capture the good, the bad, the ups and the downs of motherhood, all in her signature hilarious and witty style'

MRS HINCH

'Louise is honest and open in this book. I laughed and cried as I ploughed through the pages – I couldn't put it down and was sad when it ended! Louise is one strong, determined and inspiring woman'

KATIE PIPER

'A beautifully written, empowering story with a good dollop of Louise's inimitable wit!'

NADIA SAWALHA

'No holds barred . . . recounts the highs and lows of motherhood'

*FABULOUS*

'Candid honesty and signature wit'

*HELLO*

# Contents

# Introduction

## Aloha!

The Diet Coke is chilled, I've opened a packet of bourbon biscuits, the fairy lights are twinkling and the sofa cushions are plumped. Welcome. Come on in, the water's fine. It's just you, me and a whole book ahead of us, yasssss. Thanks so much for choosing to join me, I can't wait to share my story with you. I could just skip this introduction chapter and crack straight on, but first impressions count, don't they? You may know me already and be one of my beloved Oldie But Goldies, but it would be rude to assume so. Particularly as this book could have been gifted to you by a (discerning) present giver and you might be thinking, 'Who IS she?' – said in that same tone Nikki Grahame did on *Big Brother* in 2006. (Anyone else say that all the time and feel a bit pleased when someone 'gets it'?)

I should introduce myself properly. My name is Louise Pentland and I am a businesswoman, best-selling author, a creator of online content and keen cat lady. Not 'crazy' cat lady, just keen. Most importantly, I am a mother. That's the only title I have ever really wanted. Except maybe 'princess' too.

Being a mummy was my main goal of adulthood. Goodness knows why, because, as you will learn, I did not have the sort of blissful, fairytale upbringing that would make me think, 'This is all so brilliant! I must repeat it as soon as I am a grown-up!' The opposite, in fact: I had a sad, difficult childhood and when longed-for first-time motherhood came, it was very far from what I expected.

Don't worry though, I promise this story isn't all doom and gloom. Admittedly, it does have heartbreak, death, betrayal, divorce and depression but it also has love, hope, trust, hilarity, sass and sex (ooh-er). So, you know, something for everyone. Did I mention the sex? Let me tell you, I kissed ALL the frogs. Dad, I hope you're not reading this.

This book has been sitting around in my dusty subconscious and journals for years. From the early days of my blog, 'Sprinkle of Glitter', one of the things I loved to write about most was being a mummy. This developed with my progression into vlogging and I found a safe place to talk about the highs and lows of being a mum. I could lend a sympathetic ear to others, ask for advice in return and, for all the positive life experience I could share, there were always the fails to report back on too. I became the number one parenting vlogger in the country. Which is a lovely accolade to have but makes it sound like I know what I am talking about. Let me just say right now, on one of the very first pages I don't. I'm not a parenting expert in any way. I'm just a woman who pushed two humans out of her nether regions and shared it with the world! It's both marvellous and terrifying that you can make a career out of that these days. Eep!

There are several reasons behind my decision to write this book. The first one, slightly selfishly, is for me. Finally, from a place of happiness and safety, I have looked my life full in the face, laid bare my childhood and investigated what motherhood means to me. How much do I know? (Maybe I shouldn't have admitted back there that I'm not an expert.) Who am I and how much of me as a parent and woman has been shaped by my past experiences? Did Mum dying affect my own ability to be a mum? Did my divorce ruin my daughter's life? Should I keep the pink hair or go back to blonde? All the big questions here, my friends.

As you can imagine, the entire process has been emotional and liberating in equal measure. There were days when I couldn't face the chapter I was working on, questioned my motivation to share my story and struggled to find the words to articulate what was all stored up in my head. A lot of the rubbish bits of my life, as a coping measure, I guess, have been all scrunched up into little boxes and tucked away right at the very back. To put all those thoughts onto paper, I've had to trek back there, find that box, open it, look at it and then tell you about it. Sometimes that's been really lovely but often it's been quite brutal. There's a reason those things were packed away so tight.

There were also days when I laughed a lot as I was writing, thought about my lovely mum, my glorious girls and my dependency on rude words. Honestly, I think the biggest challenge here has been to find other words for f**cking and s**t. I don't even know if my editor will allow the starred-out versions here but let's try and sneak them in, haha! There have been big feelings, big moments and big sharing. It's warts and all. (NB: I don't actually have warts, it's just a saying.)

Spoiler alert. In case you didn't already know, my mother died early on in my life. She is the fairy godmother of my tale – a kind, loving presence who left far too soon but continues to be the driving force behind everything I do. I hope I have caught her spirit and energy between these pages, like colouring in the outline of a memory and ensuring it is preserved forever. She is a big part of who I am, probably more significant in my life by her absence than she might have been if she was still here. I won't ever know that for sure, but I do know she would have approved of my crafting obsession and maybe told me off for my filthy language (my dad certainly does).

I worry that when I mention my mum and any of the sad things in this book, that the mood will drop. Like the scene in the original *Mary Poppins* film, where Mary (played exquisitely by Julie Andrews) and Bert (the wonderful Dick Van Dyke) take the children to tea at Uncle Albert's. Albert has a special trick – laughter makes him float with happiness – and they all join in, sending them up to the ceiling, table of tea things and all. To bring them back down to earth, they think of sad things. I often turn to the LOLs to keep me buoyant when things are getting a bit bleak. That's one of my life mottos: humour always helps. We can all be a bit more Uncle Albert. Please don't take offence at my occasionally very dark sense of humour. It's sort of a 'Gotta laugh or you'll cry' kinda deal. I never mean it with malice, it's a coping mechanism.

As well as writing this book for myself and for my mum, I am writing it for my daughters. My two adorable, sassy, squidgy, big-hearted girls who inspire me every single day. They have given me the opportunity to be the best mother I can be, as well as an understanding of what being absolutely completely exhausted really is. They each have their own chapter and, at the end of the book, I have written to them – letters which I hope will stand the test of time when they read them in years to come. Who knows, this book may help them in their own parenting journeys one day, although I expect to be around to showcase fantastic granny skills if they choose to have any babies of their own.

Which brings me to my final reason for writing this book. You. This is not meant as a self-help tome, a survival guide to motherhood or one of those yummy mummy advice bestsellers (I think we all know my version of that would tank, haha!), but I have written it with you in mind. Whether you are part of the community of friends I have connected with online and shared parts of my life with over the last ten years or you are a new chum who has recently found me, I hope this book will resonate in some way. You may be a parent or assuming a parental role. Or you may be wishing for or considering motherhood. Perhaps you are struggling in your relationship with your own mother or a maternal figure in your life. You may have also experienced a devastating loss or are daunted by entry into adulthood. Or you may just like me (#ValidateMe haha) and my online life and fancy a bit of a laugh. It's not for me to pry but, whatever your reasons, I am here for you in booky pagey wordy form! I'd like my experiences to help in whatever small way they can without lecture or judgement, just a nice chit-chat, a bit of a think perhaps and best intention willing, a bit of a laugh.

Naively, I thought this book would be fairly easy to write. I have four books under my belt already so this is definitely not my first rodeo. I also, rather conceitedly, consider myself a 'natural storyteller' (I promise you it's killing me to be so complimentary to myself), but it really is one of my favourite things to do – just sit and tell a good story. Sometimes, if something particularly funny or interesting happens,

I make a little note on my phone so I can tell the story to someone with all the best bits in. I just live for that moment when you know you've said it or written it exactly how you want it to come across.

I've gone off-piste. Apologies. Back to author world: I have already written three fiction books about Robin Wilde, a plate-spinning, life-juggling, balance-seeking badass single mum and make-up artist. Any resemblance to me is entirely intended, although Robin is very much a fictional person in her own right. She and I may be on the same roller coaster of life but she has a unique way of handling situations (sometimes I wish I was as cool as her). Writing this trilogy of joy was similar to climbing a mountain (I imagine, because it's not something I have ever done or ever want to do, thank you kindly). I needed constant snacks, regular lie-downs and was often holding the map the wrong way up. I found the process exhilarating and agonising in equal measure, aiming for deadlines I knew were impossible and grateful for an incredibly understanding and supportive publisher. Once each manuscript was delivered and transformed into a proof copy I felt a huge rush of love, relief and excitement. So, I really should have been ready to write this book, but without Robin to hide behind, shit got real. (Shhh, we've snuck one in.)

I did promise not to swear too much here. Which is hard, when I am literally turning myself inside out and showing you all my organs (ew), mainly my heart (although you get to see more during the childbirth scenes – such LOLs). It helps to use bad language, it's a default of mine. Although by the time you read this, the sub-editor may have winkled them all out so do feel free to insert the odd profanity where it feels comfortable. I said many out loud while I was writing this. It is one thing to sit with a whole load of fictional characters and make them say and do what you want, it is quite another to write the truth – to write the actual raw moments onto paper. It was overwhelming and there were things that were really traumatic to relive. I felt at my most vulnerable and yet incredibly powerful at the same damned time. That's what honesty does for you. The truth, *my* truth. Maybe some of my family and friends will read this and say, 'Oh no, Louise, that's not what it was like at all, you are remembering it all wrong.' 'No,' I will say. 'For me, that is exactly what it was like.'

OK, deep breath, that's enough of that. I think we all know why we are here, although I think we are past the Diet Coke stage now. Who fancies a glass of wine instead? Or my favourite, a cheeky vodka, lime and lemonade? Let's snuggle down and begin . . .

We'll start at the very beginning, a very good place to start.*

* Heh heh, name that film . . .

# Chapter 1

## I Want To Be A Mummy: The Story of Darcy

I always wanted to have children. When anyone asked me what I hoped to be when I grew up, I would immediately reply, 'I want to be a mummy.' Not an astronaut, hairdresser or pop star – a mummy. I roleplayed parenting from an early age and, even if I do say so myself, I was very good at it. The sort of good you are when the baby is plastic, there are no other demands on your time and life has a big rosy glow about it. I don't think it was connected to knowing I wouldn't have my own mum for long. I think lots of little girls play out the same maternal fantasies. My imaginary play was full of bottle feeding, dressing the dolls in the cutest clothes and happily pushing the pram around for hours on end. When I became an adult, I knew there was more to it than that but I was sure I could capture the same feeling of complete heaven. Couldn't I?!

I met Darcy's dad at university. It was actually a bit of a fluke that I ended up there at all. Long story short – I achieved cracking GCSE results but absolutely plummeted in my A-levels. I'd moved schools for sixth form and after a decade in an all-girls school, going to a mixed environment had a rather negative impact on my grades – oops! So, I didn't make it to my first choice of university (Keele); through the 'clearing' process, I made it to Liverpool. Let me tell you, that was the BEST fluke that ever happened to me.

Anyway, I was living in halls with my friend Jessica, who now has two gorgeous children of her own too and is a great mummy friend. My first year studying psychology and biology (I absolutely love science and I'm fascinated with what makes people tick so this seemed a good course for me) at John Moore's in Liverpool went by in a flash. In my second year, Jessica and I were living in the same halls of residence but in different flats and still saw a lot of each other. One of her flatmates caught my eye. We bumped into each other in a club at the end of our second year, chatted, exchanged numbers (this was before social media, before even Facebook, so you just had to text or phone each other!) and, long story short, went into the third year of university as a couple.

We didn't spend that much time together though, as his third year involved studying abroad and I was in my final year. He was super academic and took his studies incredibly seriously, whereas I was much more laid-back about it all (I'm very much hoping Darcy takes after him with her education)! When I graduated, he had a year of his degree left so I stayed in Liverpool, moved into a house with girly mates and found a job in an office. I think I'd have stayed up there anyway, boyfriend or not, because I absolutely loved Liverpool, loved the life and friendship circles I'd built there and, sadly, didn't feel I had much to go 'home' for. One night, we went out for a lovely dinner at a little tapas restaurant in the city centre. Afterwards, we took a romantic walk along the Albert Docks, he bent down on one knee and asked me to marry him. I said yes, and felt like I was living the bloody dream.

I was 21, engaged to a man I loved and happy. We moved into our first home together, a brand-new apartment in a block called The Reach in Liverpool city centre, and had the best time, working hard during the week and going out in the evenings and at weekends, planning a wedding and talking about how much we wanted to start a family.

The year before we were due to be married, Dad told me that Mum had left me her life insurance money. It was a huge surprise and felt like she had given me a 21st birthday present, even though she wasn't there to help me celebrate. Dad attached the condition that it should be used to buy a house, preferably in Northampton (where we're from), and nothing lures a millennial more than the promise of property! So, we left Liverpool and bought a sweet little fixer-upper on a nice road for £130,000, statistically the lowest month of the lowest year of the recession (I try not to say this in a smug voice) and settled into our new jobs.

For me, there wasn't really time to miss Liverpool (though I did have a few pangs of missing the buzz of a big city). We had a wedding to plan, a house to renovate and, during lunch hours in my office receptionist job, I had a blog to write. I started my craft blog in 2009, ostensibly because I wanted to document our house project and share my DIY ideas, something I'm sure my mum would have done if blogging had existed in her day. She was a big crafter and some of my precious memories of her are at the handmade fairs she would organise. My blog, 'Beads, Buttons and A Sprinkle of Glitter', was where I uploaded my hot glue gun 'successes' and shared tips on cushion making, picture frame upcycling and the latest news on my house. It became 'A Sprinkle of Glitter' when I stepped into the world of vlogging and found my original title was too long for the URL. How brands are born, people!

We had a lot on our plates but we were young and excited, ready to embrace what came next – a baby. Everyone I knew said it takes a long time to conceive, so we figured it'd be a good idea to leave contraception to one side from about summer onwards, with the hope I'd be pregnant by

Christmas. Our wedding was booked for early September and, really stupidly, I felt confident I wouldn't be pregnant by then. I based this confidence on absolutely no research, evidence or science. Just that three out of four people had said, 'Ooh, it can take a while.' Writing it all out now, I actually feel a bit embarrassed at how ridiculous that is, but there we are! I think you believe what you want to believe sometimes.

Time went on and, in August, my uni friends (the best group of women you could ever hope to meet) organised a hen do! The morning after my raucous, drunken night out I woke up with the worst hangover and a week later I still felt awful. At first, I thought maybe this was 'age'. I was only 25 but perhaps now I'd hit the quarter-century mark it was time to ease up on the shots and stick to a respectable glass of vino. A few days later, still feeling really tired and really sick, I thought maybe this wasn't a hangover after all . . . I took a pregnancy test, saw the results and felt instant, pure joy. I also thought, 'Oh god, those shots' – the guilt, whoops!

We were both thrilled and it made our wedding day extra special, a lovely secret we were keeping, something we had only shared with our families. That was until my dad mentioned it in his father-of-the-bride speech! Hurrah/argh!

We were two happy newlyweds, pregnant with a much-wanted baby and ready with a beautifully decorated nursery. So far, so good. I hope one day when Darcy reads this, she will know how loved she was, right from being a teeny blob in my tummy.

My pregnancy was easy. I was healthy and didn't suffer from morning sickness. I was tired a lot of the time but I knew how lucky I was. It was a standard, albeit incredibly long, nine months and I revelled in it, reading about each stage. My favourite books were an NHS publication given to me by my midwife and *My Bump and Me*, a brilliant motherhood manual by Myleene Klass. I was also given a book about self-care for new mums which said stuff like, 'Make time to have a bath. Go shopping. See your friends.' Bloody hell, I thought, what are they talking about? Of course I will be doing all these things. How ridiculous.

Before having a baby it's impossible to truly understand what you are about to step into. A friend of mine moved to Singapore while I was pregnant and I breezily suggested coming out to see him in the summer with my baby. It would be eight weeks old by then and I thought I could just jump on a plane to Singapore! AHAHAHAHAHA. I would be lucky to manage getting to Tesco!

I am not a super patient person and I was absolutely desperados desperate to meet my baby, who

I found out at the second scan was a girl. YAY! I'd have been thrilled either way – all you really hope for is a healthy baby – but I think hearing she was a girl was a really special moment. I remember crying in the sonographer's office and feeling so incredibly grateful to have been given this perfect gift. My little girl! The perfect excuse for me to go big with my favourite colour and spoil her with adorable frilly dresses and lots of headbands. I was snug in a dreamy bubble of joy and anticipation. My entire life had been leading to this point and I knew that I would be the best mother with the most wonderful baby.

I didn't have my mum to prepare me for the reality and none of my friends had babies, but I didn't even think about any of that – it would all be fine, it would all be perfect. I was 25, naively forging ahead on this path with all the blind faith that women need in order to ever consider doing it in the first place. Can you sense this isn't going to go in a good direction?! Brace yourself.

My imagination created this story of how the birth and baby life would play out. I would have an adorable nursery ready with pretty dresses hung up, fresh linen folded in the drawers and soft toys lined up waiting to welcome the little one home. There would be a few twinges and off I would pop to hospital before, ouch, some pain of course (I wasn't completely deluded), maybe another ouch before the baby slipped out with a healthy yell. We would stroll home (well, drive, but then stroll happily up our little garden path) and I would spend a glorious maternity leave cuddling her all day and baking cakes when she was sleeping.

Nobody told me. In fairness, I'm not sure I really asked anybody but still . . . NOBODY TOLD ME.

So, I am telling you. With the following disclaimer:

1. I am torn between needing this part to be totally truthful and yet not wanting to scare anyone into never giving birth. If you have not yet had children you may or may not want to read on. Perhaps have a cushion ready so you can cover your face. If you have had children then you know.

2. This is my experience. Just because it happened to me does not mean it will happen to you. Everyone's birth stories are different and my second was the complete opposite to my first. You CAN have a really positive, wonderful, empowering experience. I know this because, with the right preparation (that you can easily do too), I did it.

3. I had nobody to talk to but I didn't seek anybody out. I could have gone to antenatal classes but I was too distracted with work and the house and couldn't afford any of the privately-run courses.

Maybe I didn't want hard facts; I didn't want the bubble to burst.

4. In recent years, people have been much more open about their experiences and social media is full of mummy blogs, vlogs and posts. There are those that are airbrushed and presented in a particular way but many share their reality with honesty and humour. I really freakin' wish this network had existed for my first pregnancy, but it didn't. Or if it did, it was so much in its infancy that I didn't know about it yet.

5. It is rare for things to go horribly wrong but there are still areas of pregnancy and labour that are shrouded in medical mystery. Labour and birth are astounding and our bodies are awe-inspiring.

6. The NHS is incredible, the medical profession is amazing and midwives are angels. Mistakes were made but there is no blame. They are overworked, understaffed and underpaid miracle workers. Sometimes things don't always go as we all hope. I have absolute respect to anyone who gives their time and efforts to the NHS – they are heroes. As I write the last words of this book, we are living in unprecedented times and

through a global pandemic. The NHS are heroes. Thank you.

7. Birth is a true miracle and a baby is an absolute blessing. It's the best thing I have ever, ever done and I would not change that decision for the world.

Right, now where was I? Ah yes, two weeks overdue and being sent into hospital to be induced, that's where. I didn't know that I could say no and ask to wait; I did as I was told. 'It will be OK,' I said to myself excitedly, 'I'll just go and have this induction, push the baby out and head home.' From the moment they inserted the ribbon-like pessary into my vagina and left me on a ward to crack on with it, my beautiful bubble burst. My fantasy world, not my waters, just to be clear.

Induction is a shock to the system, forcing your uterus into contractions to convince your body it is in labour. It can take a long time and even, as in my case, all day for the contractions to start – by which time my husband was sent home and I spent a sleepless night dealing with the start of labour on my own. Or not on my own, but in a room with four other women I didn't know, separated just by a curtain. Not ideal.

This was an incredibly low point. I was on a big ward with other women going through the same tumult of emotions. This could have been a bonding experience, a group of girls thrown together by circumstance who support each other through the longest night of their lives. We could have turned the experience into a boarding school dormitory, shared our labour snacks, sneaked someone out to buy more chocolate from the vending machines and told each other our secrets, knowing we would never meet again. There is a film in that where I am played by Scarlett Johansson. (True story, someone once 'kindly' told me I look like a 'quite a lot bigger Scarlett Johansson'. Cheers for that one.) OK, maybe it's more of a sitcom.

The truth was each of us was trapped in our own private world of pain and mental anguish, trying to be brave, calm, quiet, to cope with the fear of the unknown and be undemanding of the hospital staff. This was not the time for a group hug and rallying call of togetherness. I think back on this time and I can see the lost opportunity but I don't think any of us could have connected across the bed pans and birthing balls. I was surrounded by people and yet I felt so alone, marooned in my agony. It was exposing, these waves of pain and fear. I was almost embarrassed by it and wanted to hide away from the world, back into a corner and just be peacefully alone in it all. The flimsy protection of the hospital curtain was not enough, but it would have to do.

When my husband returned in the morning, I was shattered but relieved to see him. It also meant that our baby was on its way, it was all going to be OK and we would soon meet her. As the day wore on and the pain grew more intense, so did my horror. I was struggling with lack of sleep, regular contractions and far too many invasive examinations. That's another thing they don't tell you, that midwives and random doctors will stop off and stick their hands up your vagina. You do actually have a choice in this but it was never worded like I did. 'OK, let's see where we are,' actually means, 'Okie cokie, time for your sober fingering from someone you don't really know'. I now know that I could have said, 'Is this absolutely needed? Are there other ways you can check mine and the baby's health? If it's not vital to our health, I don't want you to do that, please.' Sadly, I was ill-prepared and ill-informed. This broke any last image I clung to of a beautiful labour. Morale was pretty low.

By lunchtime on the second day, I was still not fully dilated and stuck in a queue for a midwife-run birthing suite. Even knowing I was at the top of that queue did not help; I was desperate for privacy and drugs. I couldn't have gas and air on the main ward so I took the paracetamol offered even though it felt like an insult and it didn't make the slightest difference. I didn't want to 'take the edge' off the pain, I wanted a private room to labour with my husband and meet my daughter. Tough. The ward was overrun and it was the corner of the ward with a curtain for me. Woo!

By 3pm I was in a birthing suite, on my 31st hour of labour and begging for serious drugs. It was then that the fun really started. *I am writing that in a sarcastic tone of voice.* There was a three-hour wait for the anaesthetist because they were understaffed so an epidural was not an option, but did I fancy a little shot of pethidine in my leg? You bet your sweet ass I did. That midwife could have said literally anything and if she'd added the words 'pain relief' to it, I'd have taken it. I wasn't coping well with my pain because, as I mentioned, I hadn't prepared for this experience at all. Lesson fully learnt for next time! So, I took the injection that I'd never heard of and knew nothing about in my leg and hoped it would all be better. Except it turned out that I was allergic to pethidine so, rather than being my saviour, it added another layer of misery to the proceedings. Fabulous!

After a period of excessive vomiting and the threat of dehydration, the medical team decided they needed to hook me up to an IV fluid drip. I don't like those little needle things in my hand but I gave in to it because it was spoken about as though this was for the best, and when you're incredibly vulnerable and trying to protect the also incredibly vulnerable human life inside you, you just kind of do what you're told. Interestingly though, I don't know exactly what happened at this point because I was concentrating on the lion that was in the room, weighing out Parma Violets on old-fashioned grocery scales. I was hallucinating, literally off my head on the drugs and the pain. Things weren't going well.

The nurse missed my vein when she was inserting the needle for the drip so there was blood everywhere. She tried again, but this time something else went wrong (I don't know if the needle went into the wrong place or what) and fluid made my hand swell up and turned my fingers into bananas. I knew they weren't actual bananas; I wasn't hallucinating that badly. They tried the other hand and the same thing happened again. The same bloody thing! So both hands had useless banana fingers that I couldn't bend or pick anything up with, I was still being sick (I'd ruined all my own clothes by now, so I just had a hospital gown draped over my bare body), was severely dehydrated and asking my bewildered husband how much longer till we got to Cornwall. Was this really what labour was like? Don't answer that.

There were five more hours of hell to wade through, including: trying to wee in a cardboard bedpan in front of my husband; trying to maintain a 'normal' conversation about my degree with the kind student midwife who I was left alone with because my main midwife was looking after two labouring women at once, and the drugs making me feel so hot but, for some reason, not being allowed a fan on. By this point, my longed-for baby was 'taking too long' to arrive and in distress. Her heart rate had dropped so they attached a monitor to her head (via my vagina), broke my waters and told me to start pushing. Time was of the essence or I would be carted off for an emergency Caesarean. Nothing makes you feel more relaxed than that as a threat over you.

As out of it as I was, I could feel the tension in the room. The midwives were not happy, there were people in and out checking the monitor, talking over my exhausted, wired-up body. I don't remember anyone talking to me properly except my husband, who was kind throughout. I feel it's important to include that part, not for me as the author or you as the reader, but for Darcy. If she one day reads this, I want her to know that despite all the hardship around her birth, her parents were both happy to have her.

It took just five pushes – well, feet in stirrups, a brutal episiotomy, a big vaginal tear and five pushes – and healthy nine-pound baby Darcy arrived into the world! She was handed straight to me. She was the softest, warmest, most beautiful little thing, the reassuring weight of her on my chest and, in that instant, I thought, 'This is bliss.' Then I threw up all over myself. Brilliant.

At this point in the story, can I remind you about my earlier caveats? This next bit is not for the faint-hearted. It is important for me to share it but you may not want to read it, which is totally cool. I can let you know when you can open your eyes again.

For the rest of you, imagine an episode of *Holby City*. As the placenta came out I began to bleed and didn't stop. I was haemorrhaging from my vagina as someone hit the emergency buzzer and the doors swung open, exposing me to the corridor and everyone beyond. People were rushing in and out and I was there in the middle of the drama, legs still in stirrups, vagina on show for all the world to see. They were trying to stop the bleeding, swabbing me and shouting instructions to each other. I had the weirdest sensation that I was swimming, slipping in and out of consciousness. One of the midwives was saying, 'Hold your baby, hold your baby,' like a distant mantra. I wasn't sure I could hang onto her, everything was behaving strangely, my arms felt really limp and please don't forget #bananahands. 'Look at your baby,' she kept repeating and I thought, 'This is it. I am going to die in childbirth and my daughter will be left without a mother, just like I was.

That's why they want me to look at her – I'm never going to see her again.' My vision was blurry, I couldn't see Darcy's face. I thought I would die having never looked at her properly. It was one of the very worst moments of my life. As I type this, I can remember it all so vividly and I want to cry. The thought of never seeing Darcy's beautiful little face is a thought I never want to have again. This is the end of the paragraph, because any more detail and I might fully break.

I lost two hours that night. Unconscious, asleep, I'm not sure what happened, but I woke up at 10.30pm with a patchy memory of events. Darcy's dad had put a nappy on her and was holding her – she looked so small and safe in his arms. A nurse came in to clean me up and check my stitches. I couldn't sit up properly and felt so insecure on the bed, like it would break and I would fall off and that would be the end for my sore damaged body. I felt terrible. Ill, tired, violated, confused by those lost hours and in shock.

Someone we vaguely knew who worked in the hospital came in to see us. It was a sweet gesture of congratulation but it took everything I had left not to shout at her to get the eff out. Now was not the time for small talk and chit-chat! I didn't even have a pair of sodding knickers on! Give me a shred of dignity, please!

By 2am I was 'well' enough to attempt to go to the toilet but stitches and nerves stopped me, so I was sent back to bed to have a catheter fitted. This involved revisiting the scene of recent bloodshed, having a tube put up my urethra and the midwife asking Darcy's dad to put her down for a minute so he could hold the light and shine it on the war zone. Nobody asked if I was OK with all of that. In that moment, I had never ever felt so disgusting, so vile. I am not sure how relationships ever survive these things.

For those with a nervous disposition, you can open your eyes now. To conclude this part of the birth story, I can say that what was supposed to be the best day of my life was most definitely the worst. The only mercy from the whole experience was that I didn't poo myself and when *that* is all you have to cling to, then it's a good measure of a terrible day. Darcy was the saving grace of the entire debacle, of course. My perfect, beautiful baby.

I was physically and mentally battered. A hospital porter unceremoniously dumped me in a wheelchair and whizzed me back to the ward, clutching Darcy, while her father was sent home. It was the early hours of the morning and I hadn't slept for two days. I was alone with a new baby and no idea what to do. In addition, I still had my banana fingers, which made being useful pretty damn hard, and my vagina was in literal bits. Moving around was agony.

When Darcy started to cry, I was terrified. I cried too. I had no idea how to breastfeed, change a nappy or comfort her, and I couldn't even reach the carefully packed nappy bag. I rang the buzzer for the nurse, who told me to stick her on the breast. Ever tried that with banana fingers and a breast you've never fed from before? Well don't, because it's almost impossible. I attempted it, Darcy calmed and I put her back in her cot. She immediately started screaming again. I was in a shared ward, half-delirious and worried about waking the other new mums and their babies. I buzzed the nurse again. 'You would feel a lot better,' she said, 'if you tried to be independent.' I sat bolt upright for the remaining hours of the night, clumsily holding onto Darcy and waiting for her dad to return to us at 9am.

Throughout my time in hospital, I felt a little like I was in an old-fashioned horror film. One where everyone around you behaves completely normally and has no idea what you are making a fuss about. Midwives and health visitors would pop in with leaflets and reassuring words. Some tried to encourage open curtains on the ward, 'So we can all be sociable, ladies.' Just because we had given birth at the same time did not mean that we needed to be friends. I wasn't Scarlett Johansson in a film about a labour ward where all the women become lifelong friends after shared traumas; I was Louise Pentland, reeling from the experience, still trying to work out what had happened to me and how I was going to cope with a new baby. I didn't want my tits exposed to an entire ward while I tried to get my head around breastfeeding. It was also no help to know that the woman in the bed next to me had just had a lovely water birth with lots of aromatherapy oils. She was keen to share her story and I was not keen to hear it. I smiled and nodded politely, made an excuse about needing to get changed, hoisted myself off the bed (no mean feat) and firmly shut the curtains.

Although I felt like I was in the hospital a lifetime, I also only have really hazy memories of it. My friend Marie says she forgets all the bad things that ever happen to her, not on purpose but her brain just does it to keep her going, to keep surviving. I remember the night I arrived on the ward with Darcy, the early morning wake-up from the Bounty Woman giving me a bunch of advertising leaflets in a folder (cheers for that), only being allowed one set of grandparents to come and see Darcy on the ward and the Big Wee.

I'd told the nurses I wanted to go home and I recall one saying that before she'd discharge me, she wanted to see that I could do 'a big wee'. I now know I wasn't a prisoner and had the right to leave at any point but, as we've established, back then I was clueless. Well, I've never drunk so much water in my life. I gulped down about two litres, shuffled to the bathroom with a carboard bowl, did the Big Wee, shuffled to the nurses' office, presented said Big Wee and, *voila*, I was 'allowed' home. Who knew that a giant whizz was a key that unlocked the door? Bloody hell.

It was a relief to go home but then the endless stream of visitors started. I retold and relived the birth story many times over. I thought I should be honest about it and not give it a Disney makeover. Wasn't that what everyone did, tell the truth, however horrific? I could see people looking at me, probably imagining my vagina ripping as I talked. It was like being an animal in the zoo, I felt exposed.

The first few days with Darcy were beyond awful. She cried all the time – one night, I just cried with her. We scraped through the days on a never-ending round of visitors and tea and cake (I don't even like tea!) and then at night she'd cry and cry and cry. I kept feeding and feeding, changing and soothing, but it made little difference.

After a week, the midwife came over and weighed Darcy. She had lost 10 per cent of her body weight, which meant an immediate return to hospital. I dreaded going back but Darcy was suffering – she was severely dehydrated as she wasn't feeding properly, so we immediately headed back into hospital.

I was weighed down with the most awful guilt. I had failed. I had been hopeless at breastfeeding and I hadn't done things right. That's why she had been crying so much. She had tried to feed and then given up because she wasn't getting much milk. I had assumed that meant she was full but as soon as I put her down, she would start to cry again. She was desperately hungry and I hadn't helped her. Rationally, I knew I couldn't have known that, but when you're that tired and that broken, you're not thinking rationally, you're just ripping yourself to shreds for being a shit mother and worrying that everyone will know you have no clue what you're doing, and maybe they'll take the baby away or something hideous like that.

Back in the hospital, we were surrounded by posters with the slogan 'breast is best'. I couldn't have felt any worse about my inability to look after her. Formula feeding had not been an option; it did not fit into my vision of motherhood and all the antenatal literature reiterated that. Luckily, one kind consultant, a senior professional, cut through it all. In no uncertain terms he said, 'Your baby is starving. Fed is best.' I have never forgotten that or the feeling of relief when we gave her the first bottle of formula and she gulped it down. We stayed in the hospital for a couple of nights and it was something of a turning point. We were free from visitors (except the medical staff, who were all so sweet with her), Darcy was feeding well and finally, we could all sleep. Things became a little easier.

Those early days of motherhood were bewildering. I loved Darcy so much I would have run into a burning building to save her, but I couldn't feel that instant bond that people refer to. That 'wave' of love. I had been in so much pain, completely terrified and trying to fall in love with her while everything around me was falling apart. In the early days, with so many visitors, she was passed around and I only got to hold her when she was breastfeeding unsuccessfully.

I remembered a woman I had met as I was taking a labour-inducing walk around the hospital all those days before. She was carrying a six-month-old and smiled at me with a mix of empathy and encouragement. 'I've been where you are now,' she said, 'but I can tell you it's all worth it in the end.' Is it, I kept thinking. When will it all be worth it, because it sure as hell isn't right now?! Others would say, 'Isn't this the most magical time?' and I would smile and nod but inside I was yelling 'WHAT THE HELL ARE YOU TALKING ABOUT?!' What on earth was I missing? This is what I had been born to be. Not an astronaut, hairdresser or pop star, just a lovely mummy. How hard could it be? It felt like I had lived a nightmare of blood, gore and now exhaustion. Motherhood was propaganda and I had fallen for it, hook, line and sinker.

We were gradually settling into a routine. A safe monotony of sleeping, feeding, bathing and playing. As the haze of the early days lifted, I found myself thinking back more to the labour and birth. Every time I dwelt on it I would cry and with each retelling of the story I would feel physically sick. I felt dirty, remembering myself covered in blood, and it revolted me. I disgusted myself.

To begin with, I shared my thoughts with the visiting midwives. Not the darkest of those thoughts about myself – for example, when I wanted to get in a boiling hot shower and scrub my skin till it was raw – just the part about flashbacks and crying. They called it the baby blues and said it would disappear after a couple of weeks – 'All perfectly normal.' I waited and the depression waited with me. Then it was suggested by my midwife that I take antidepressants. 'No way,' I thought, 'I don't need medication, I just need something to wipe the bad memories.' I'm not sure why I was so averse to medication, something inside me just knew it wasn't post-natal depression.

I tried a six-week counselling course. The counsellor meant well and did lots of reassuring listening and nodding but it was of no practical help. Darcy's dad speaks Spanish and he said the Spanish word for birth is *nacimiento* which, roughly translated, means 'to give light' and that stuck with me. It was the most reassuring thought and I clung to it. What I had done wasn't disgusting, I had given light.

As well as those low lows, there were also a few high highs. In the midst of this time, Darcy was my joy, the loveliest thing, my absolute gift. I remember vividly really enjoying taking her out in her pram. I had a Silver Cross Deluxe Sleepover in the shade 'sugared almond' as a gift from her paternal grandparents and I was SO proud of it. The first time I took her out was to Milton Keynes shopping centre when she was 12 days old and pushing her through John Lewis felt like such a surreal experience. I felt like I'd really made it.

I loved dressing her in sweet outfits and putting tiny little headbands over her peach fuzz hair. I used to sit her on my old cream sofas and film little 'Baby OOTDs'* and think they were so fun.

I remember getting so much joy from just taking photos of her. I didn't think there was anything

---

* Outfit of the Day for anyone not on Instagram!

at all more beautiful in the entire world than this sweet baby. I took photos in flowers, photos by Christmas trees, photos on my lap, photos on blankets, photos everywhere. I even entered her into a baby beauty contest (which she won) because I was just so certain she was the most stunning thing on the planet. Of course, every mother is biased and all our babies are beauties but I still think she's absolutely gorgeous.

As she grew a little older, the flashbacks settled and we found our feet. She moved on from her bottle feeds to real food (with a big love for Marmite sandwiches) and we started living life properly again.

I stopped sharing my fears as nobody seemed to understand me. I felt awful that the fuss I was making could have an impact on Darcy. God forbid they may think I was an unfit mother and try and take her away. I suppressed all the feelings of violation and consoled myself with the fact that I would never have to go through it again. Darcy was perfect, she filled our hands and hearts, I didn't need another baby and there was no way I was going to suffer that agony again. Years later, I did revisit my anguish with several medical professionals who independently said it sounded like I had suffered from PTSD. It was a relief to hear that and the symptoms of the disorder were very familiar to me.

## How to Survive Life After Birth

1. You do not need to share your birth story if you are not happy to. Just because other people do doesn't mean you should, particularly if your experience has been traumatic. It is OK to keep it private. Thank them for asking and say it was incredible, unexpected, terrifying, mind-blowing (whatever word encapsulates it for you), but it is not something you want to go into detail about. I wish I hadn't been so open about my story at the time, although now I want to share it to help others.

2. Limit visitors. Everyone is desperate to meet the baby and congratulate you, which is a lovely thing. If you consider your family and all your friends just popping around for a cuppa, that can take up every day for a rather long time. It's a time when you should stay in bed if you need to, breast- or bottlefeed your baby without an audience, strengthen the bonding process and start to find some sort of routine. Constant visitors make that impossible and pile on the pressure. Before you give birth, manage everyone's expectations. Tell them you will let them know when you are ready. Which may

be within hours of giving birth or may be several days or weeks later. Whatever it is, you need to be in control. Your birth, your baby, your rules. *Sassy S click*

3. Take help when it is offered. My Aunty Judith was a great support, coming round with food after the baby was born, being available to hold her while I had a shower and counselling me through low moments. My stepmother Tina encouraged me to take some time for myself and babysat so I could go to the cinema on my birthday. She reminded me that I'm still a person and it's fine to still enjoy myself as well as being a mummy.

4. Talk to the midwives about how you are feeling and take advantage of any practical help they offer. There is a brilliant initiative in the UK called Meet the Matron, where you book to sit down with a maternity matron and go through your notes. Often in the middle of labour you have no idea what is happening to you or why. It was life-changing for me. I sat with a medical professional who went through my labour notes, explaining why those decisions were made and helped me understand and rationalise my experience. It took me six years to do this because I didn't know it existed but, honestly, it was a total game changer.

5. Remember how you are feeling is a reflection on your own mental health and not how you are feeling about your beautiful baby. It's alright to feel like you really don't like a situation. I didn't love those early days of motherhood but I absolutely did love Darcy. I was worried if I said I wasn't loving things, it would all be muddled and I'd sound like I didn't love her. I shouldn't have been.

6. Keep an eye on the new mums around you. Just because they say they are fine doesn't mean they really are. When my friends have their first baby, I let them know I am ready to pop over when they are ready and come prepared with a big bag of McDonald's and a listening ear. They may or may not want to talk (see my first point) but I always ask them how they are. Not the baby, or how the birth was, but how they are feeling. I offer my time and say go for a nap, have a shower, answer phone messages, scroll aimlessly on Instagram, anything you want or need to do, and I will hold the baby. Nobody needs another blanket or a tiny hat with matching mittens, they just want two hands back or a bit of a nice sleep.

During this tumultuous time, I continued to vlog. I know that seems weird considering everything I have just said, but it was an absolute sanity saver. A positive way to focus on my new life. I could act like a functioning person on the outside, go to London to attend events and be distracted from my own thoughts. It was the only time I really felt like me.

I never considered vlogging as a career until Darcy was almost one and the end of my maternity leave was looming. If I went back to my office job part-time, I would earn around £500 a month and most of this would go on childcare, which seemed ridiculous. I enjoyed my office job but it was a means to an end. I would also be going back to an unstable environment as I was PA to a manager who had recently resigned and the position had been made redundant. There was no clear plan for my return and I suspected I would be doing office admin and reception. The thought of leaving my baby to do a job that didn't cover my costs, inspire me or offer long-term security was bleak. I needed to do something else, fast.

What if I could earn £500 through my online life without having to leave the house and, more importantly, Darcy? I would be swapping one unstable job for another unstable job but at least I was in control of this one. If I worked hard I would directly benefit. The flexibility and thought of enjoying what I was doing were the key factors in my decision. It was worth a shot.

So, with renewed energy, I uploaded weekly blogs and vlogs, embraced just-launched Instagram and worked the metaphorical room. It was such an exciting time as this style of media was so new, nobody knew exactly where it was heading so you could be brave and experimental with content. I started working with sponsors and brands, became part of the 'YouTube Brit Crew' (not a name I made myself and not something you applied to, I just happened to become friends with a group of people who seemed to be named that by the media) and signed with a management company who would help me develop and continue in a career I loved. Things on that side were really looking up!

Darcy was the easiest baby ever. She was placid, content, slept and travelled really well. Her gentle spirit shone out. I had no mum to help me, nobody around to babysit much (though I did lean on Tina a lot, who was amazing, I didn't feel comfortable asking for too many favours. I felt like I had made the choice to have Darcy so I should take care of her. Accepting help is a skill I've learnt over time) and couldn't afford extra help so she came everywhere with me. We would often jump on the train together and head to various events. I remember a particularly fancy dinner at Harrods when I turned up with Darcy and offered a breezy, 'Sorry, I don't have childcare,' by way of explanation and everyone seemed totally fine. Darcy was a bit of a fixture at the work things I went to. When I filmed my videos at home, I would set up the tripod, sit Darcy under it with her toys and she would play quietly while I worked away, building this exciting career. It was amazing!

The other powerful thing about my new career was the community I found online. They were a complete tonic. I didn't have any mummy friends around me but I quickly built up a network of other bloggers and vloggers and a great audience of kind people who left supportive comments. They say it takes a village to bring up a child and these people were my village.

Of course, the online world can be hard to navigate. As a vlogger, I put myself out there – a new mum trying to do her best. I didn't share my struggle directly as I didn't understand it myself or know how to communicate what I was feeling then, but I felt the encouragement and support from those who followed me. In turn, I followed other parent vloggers, watching snippets of their lives with daily social media updates that made me feel less lonely. I still value and need those I follow as I move through each phase of mothering. Like any village, there are always the tricky people, the ones who don't want you to succeed, who revel in pointing out your failings and take pleasure in your discomfort. I have had more than my fair share of that but am generally able to mute them in my head and take the good from the people who are genuinely on the journey with me. The good eggs.

When Darcy was a toddler, her dad and I realised we had drifted apart. We tried to work it out but, by the time she was three, we had decided to separate. I had never judged anyone before in this situation but I felt ashamed, vulnerable, like everyone might think it was my fault that the marriage had broken down. Nobody ever said that to me but I was paranoid they thought it. We could have stayed together longer but it wouldn't have been a happy environment for any of us. There was no big drama, betrayal or fury, just an acceptance that it was better to be two happy parents apart. Neither of us was prepared to be the 'every other weekend' parent. We were equal parents so we split custody fairly, straight down the middle.

It was 2014, I was now a single mother and I yearned for my own mum more than ever. I wanted a reassuring maternal figure to step in and take the weight when it was too heavy for me to bear. The shape of her loss took on a new, overwhelming perspective. Suddenly she became a woman who hadn't just missed out on her daughter but her granddaughter too.

# Chapter 2

# My Lovely Mum

I only knew Mum for the first seven years of my life but she is a huge, irreplaceable part of me and my motherhood story with my own daughters. My memories of her are precious as I have so few of them, but close family have shared their stories over the years, creating a clearer picture of the woman she was and how much I am like her, which is the greatest compliment to me.

Oof, this is such a hard thing to write about. I use humour a lot when I speak about the loss of Mum, in fact, I have a new term for it – 'death-iquette', an etiquette for the grieving, if you will. A language and humour that you share with those who have been through a similar experience and know the power of being able to laugh in the toughest times. I find that people who have been in your shoes understand death-iquette the most. They laugh at the 'joke' but also understand the underlying pain. My friend Marie in America 'gets it'. Her wonderful mother passed away a few years ago and suddenly Marie and I were in a weird club together that nobody really wants to be in – but once you find yourself in it you're glad of the company. Humour helps as you can't be sad all the time, it's exhausting. It doesn't mean things don't affect me or that I'm not sad that she's gone. I cried when I thought about the memories I wanted to include in this book, the awful things that are important to tell but hard to write down. I hope I can capture her beautiful spirit in these pages, to keep my memories alive and pass on to my girls. She was a generous, passionate, creative woman with a determined core and streak of unpredictability and I am so immensely proud of her.

Mum was born Diana Jane but hated the Diana bit of her name so always insisted on being called Jane. She was initially the middle child of three girls (her dad went on to have more children in his next marriage) – Judith, her older, wilder sister and Rose, the younger, studious one. It sounds like Mum was a bit of both, possibly more on the naughty side – although she was very good at never being caught.

Her parents broke up when the girls were still small; her father was a wrong 'un and had treated her mum, my gran, very badly. While him leaving was no great loss to the family, it left them struggling to make financial ends meet. Not a great position to be in at any time and definitely not in the 1960s when there was shame associated with divorce. Mum's dad didn't notice – he married the woman it turned out he had been having an affair with and started a new family. With his new wife (a nice lady, who I've met lots) he had two more children – Jackie (who is in my life) and a son who lives abroad and I don't know.

It was tough for Gran, raising three girls, working in a shop, trying to keep them all going without any additional support. They didn't have a lot of treats and they certainly didn't live the life my girls do now with lots of lovely holidays, toys and fun days out. Unsurprisingly, Mum left school early. She wasn't academic and needed to earn some money to help Gran, so she took a secretarial job in a local office. This is where she met my dad. At the time, Mum was engaged to a soldier, Graham, who was about to whisk her off to live in Germany in army barracks. The wedding was planned, the cake had even been bought but Dad was keen, refused to give up and relentlessly wooed her.

She hadn't liked him at first. Legend has it that he would come into the office for meetings and annoy her, once going as far as stealing a Mars Bar off her desk. She hated him. Then she didn't (that was some wooing, Dad – well done!). She left Graham and the prospect of life in Germany as an army wife and she began dating Dad. 'But what happened to the wedding cake?' I hear you ask. Well, she kept it and ate it with Gran and her sisters around the kitchen table. We are not a family to waste cake!

Mum and Dad married and moved into their first home together in 1979. The house was number 39 in a street with 'Green' in its name. Exactly 40 years later, in 2009, the first house I bought was also number 39 in a street with 'Green' in its name. I loved the serendipity of this, a little message from Mum. I know it took Mum a long time to conceive and she suffered a miscarriage before becoming pregnant with me. When they moved to Leeds for Dad's job, she found out she was pregnant with me and that, dear reader, is where I was born, on the 28th April 1985. Ta-da! Hello, world!

We moved back to Northampton when I was two but I don't have loads of memories before Mum was diagnosed with cancer. I was only five and the next two years until she died were full and vibrant, despite what was happening medically. Perhaps because she was actively creating memories for me in case we didn't have long together. The memories I do have, I cherish. I keep them like gemstones in a treasure box because they are so special to me and I never want to lose them.

I remember my mum being the archetypal 1980s chick. Tall and slim, with dark hair, glasses and frosted pink lip gloss, she loved sweatshirts and matching slacks with an ironed crease. Her sleeves would be pushed up to the elbow, making the fabric bunch up around her upper arm, looking like an extra from *Miami Vice*. Or she wore pleated midi skirts, a loose blazer, thin denier tights and a low heel, her wardrobe and hairstyle both inspired by the original 'influencer' and absolute style icon, Princess Diana.

She had the most beautiful long, slim fingers and manicured nails, talented hands that crafted and collected gorgeous things. She ran a craft business, not only selling her own handmade products but organising fairs for other creators to gather and sell their wares. I used to keep her company on those weekends and they were some of my happiest times with her and our wider group of family and friends. My Aunt Judith had a stall of her knitted garments. She could tackle anything, as proven by the photo of me in knitted skirt, top and hat, finished off with a pair of shiny patent shoes. At least she didn't try and knit me the shoes . . .

I would hang out with Judith's son, my cousin Daniel, who was two years younger but the greatest friend (and still is). Sometimes our pal Richard would join us too – his mum Jill was my mum's best friend and she ran the best ever cake stall. Mum loved her and renamed her Jilly Willy Botty Bare Bum, a name that has stuck with her ever since and makes me laugh whenever I say it out loud. My funny mum, Aunty Judith and Jilly Willy Botty Bare Bum were the best girl gang and tagging along with them felt amazing! It was a time full to the brim with laughter and adventure. I would often wake up in the back of Mum's white Vauxhall Astra (she was an early bird so would carry me to the car in my jimjams with a big blanket) with a foil parcel of honey toast and a note, then we'd be loaded up and on our way somewhere exciting. Mum loved a day trip – something I now do too!

When we weren't out and about with the girl gang or setting up craft fairs, there were always waifs and strays at our house. I just thought that was normal. Mum's heart was huge and her capacity to help was endless. She was close to her half-sister, Jackie, who was much younger than her and often found herself in a pickle with boyfriends. Jackie would turn up with her bin bags of clothes and a sorry tale, staying with us for weeks on end. I know my mum loved Jackie so much. She loved having her come to stay and, right till the end of her life, she was a massive support. I feel like Jackie has returned all that love to me over the years and done so many amazing things that Mum would love. She let us host Darcy's first birthday in a tearoom she was running and, a year before that, she gave me her old car to run around in. Mum would be so proud of Jackie.

Mum couldn't bear to see anyone in trouble or suffering and her concern stretched beyond the family. Once my dad returned from a business trip to Moscow, where he had been invited to lecture at a computer conference, bringing back a story of the translator he had worked with out there. Elaine, a Russian single mum with two young girls, was living in abject poverty and he was horrified by it. He wanted to do something to help and talked to Mum. She couldn't bear it and they agreed that they would invite her to England for a few days as a little break from her life. I'm told there were a LOT of problems with visas, but after a lot of phone calls with the Russian and British Embassies and a stroke of luck with one of the officials realising Elaine was actually in the building at the time on a translating job and saying, 'Elaine, your wish is granted,' she went home, gathered her two children and flew out that night!

Elaine, her daughters Marsha (who was eight at the time) and Katya (five at the time) came and spent the most magical Christmas with us. It was 1990 and things in Moscow were VERY different then. Elaine explained how they'd had to queue outside supermarkets and the shelves were bare. One of my memories is of Mum driving us all to Tesco. We went in and Elaine broke down in tears of joy because she'd never seen so much food. Mum and Dad made sure she had the best Christmas of her life. My Great-Aunt Edna made us three little ballerina outfits and everyone rallied round to sort Christmas presents and treats for them.

When they went home, Mum was devastated, having formed a real bond. That April, she went over to Moscow and set upon a mission to bring them back – this time for good! She jumped through every legal hoop, worked through all the red tape, said her and Dad would be financial guarantors, found Elaine work and housing – and in no time at all, the Russians were moving!

As a mother myself now, I can't imagine how all this must have felt for the Russian lady who'd trusted in an English woman she barely knew and was seeing all these things for the first time. It makes me incredibly grateful to be able to give my daughters the lives they have.

The girls came to school with me and it seems crazy now but, at the time, I just accepted the situation. Mum was insistent that Elaine could build a new and better life in the UK and continued to support her, even trying to find her a husband, Tinder-style, by taking a photo of her in a bluebell wood and sending the picture to the local *Chronicle* and *Echo*. The letter headlined, 'Glamorous Russian Looking for Love'. I am not sure if Elaine ever found a husband, but they moved to London soon after and when Mum died, we lost touch. I often wonder how they are doing and am still amazed by Mum's bravery and determination. Erin Brockovich make room for Jane Pentland! Also, side note, if you know my long-lost Russian 'family', please contact me! I'd love to talk to them again!

Mum was always putting other people first and stepping into situations with the best intentions. We lived on a hill which backed onto a main road and a steady stream of traffic. I remember it so vividly. One day, I was in the spare bedroom at the back of the house and I was lining all my soft toys up with little plastic instruments to make a band. I heard what I thought was lightning and rolling thunder but was in fact a terrible crash between a lorry and bus. The bus careered down the hill and straight into our neighbours', Stan and Pam's (honestly their actual names) bungalow, which was right next door to us. I heard afterwards that the driver of the bus deliberately steered (as best he could) the bus into their house and not ours because he could see my swing set in our garden and assumed children must live there. Unlucky for Stan and Pam's brickwork but so lucky for us, as both Mum and I were right at the back of the house and the ending of this story could have been very different!

As soon as the bus hit, Mum bounded out and straight onto the bus, pulling people off and bringing them into our sitting room. It was like a makeshift A&E department with the walking wounded sat bleeding and shocked, waiting for the ambulances to arrive. There was blood everywhere, Stan and Pam were stunned but, amazingly, nobody was seriously hurt! Dad came home to the tail end of the drama, Mum busy and calm in the midst of it all. She was awarded a police medal for her courageous and swift actions that day and we all dined out on that tale for years!

I often ask myself, why her? Why would someone so generous, so loving, so charismatic, be taken so soon? It still doesn't make sense.

I was at school, aged only about five years old, in the playground at the end of the day, waiting to be collected by Mum. She didn't arrive, which I knew was a bit odd, so I went to wait at the school reception, as was the procedure if your mum or dad were late. Dad came in to collect me, which was also unusual – it still really sticks out to me all these years later. When we went out to the car, I saw he had parked in the staff car park, next to the teachers' cars. I knew this was breaking school rules and I was horrified – he was going to be in big trouble for that. I wondered if Mr Povey, our headteacher, would come out and tell my dad off. I remember feeling so panicked about this and frustrated that my dad didn't seem to care about this huge rule break.

We walked over to the car and Mum was sitting in the passenger seat, crying. Right there, still standing in the car park, Dad said they had driven straight from the hospital. He told me Mum had a disease called cancer and she was ill. I couldn't really comprehend what he was saying and I didn't for one minute think she was going to die. I was more worried about leaving the car park before we were spotted and sent to the headmaster's office. It's a painful memory to dwell on now. Tiny me, in my school uniform, desperate to abide by the rules. My parents, given that awful diagnosis, before driving over to collect me. My mum sobbing in the car. None of us having any idea of what would happen next.

It was a two-year battle. Mum had found a lump in her breast way before the diagnosis and had been pushing the doctor to test her but was told it was just a cyst. There were months of appointments and delays before the biopsy results finally revealed her biggest fears. I spoke to Dad about it a long while after, wondering if he had ever thought to sue the doctor who had so flippantly dismissed her worries. He said he wasn't cross, there was no point holding onto the anger as it wouldn't bring Mum back. 'The doctor is just human,' he said. 'She was unlucky, these things happen.'

While we still had Mum we made sure we had some really special holidays. We went to Lanzarote, a big family trip of aunts and cousins, my mum in the loving centre of it all. It must have been agony for them, such a bittersweet time together, but I just remember it as a fantastic week in the sun, playing with my cousin Daniel. My attitude was that this was time with Mum and, at some point, there would be time without Mum, but I was too young to understand the impact of this. Mum embraced every alternative therapy as well as the traditional methods but, in the end, this was one battle she wasn't going to win.

Before things deteriorated, we had one last hurrah and went to Disneyland Paris, or 'Euro Disney' as it was known then. I still didn't know how serious things were with Mum's health and just remember it being the most wonderful couple of days. We walked through Alice in Wonderland's maze and saw all the giant figures of cards painting roses red and the evil Queen shouting, 'Off with their heads'; we went on the Dumbo ride (always riding in the elephant with a pink hat on, that was my little tradition) and we met all sorts of Disney characters.

To me, it was a day of magic with my mummy and daddy. To them, it must have been torture, knowing this was our last special experience together. I'm (gratefully) able to take my girls to Disney a lot now and every single time I step through those whimsical arches that lead onto Main Street, with those spectacular views of the castle, I whisper a little hello up to Mum in heaven, knowing she'll be standing silently beside me, loving us all so much.

As she grew progressively worse, she became bedridden at home. To give her a break from the headaches and sunlight, her curtains were always drawn, which I hated. They were a dark maroon colour and when the light shone through them, the whole room glowed a deep red colour that I found so unsettling.

It was a relief filled with sadness when she was moved to Northampton General Hospital and then soon after to a hospice. I had no idea what this meant – I asked why she was moving, presuming hospital and hospice were the same thing, a place where ill people were looked after and made better. She told me the phone was too noisy in the ward she was on so she had asked to be moved somewhere quieter, where she could relax. This made perfect sense, I was happy she was going to be somewhere quiet where she could recover and then come home to me. Nobody told me what a hospice actually was. I don't think I would have understood it if they had. For me, the Cynthia Spencer Hospice was a joyous place. I renamed it Marks & Spencer Hospice and every time we went, I would singsong our arrival into the intercom before being buzzed in.

Mum had a nice room with a connecting bedroom where we could stay over. There was often a theme to our visit: cakes one night or felt-tip colouring – a strong memory I have of her still. My aunts and cousins would turn up, the younger of us racing up and down the halls on bed trolleys. I know I was spoilt during this time, my 15-year-old cousin Andrew spent his pocket money on a doll that blew bubbles for me. So much family love around us all, but one terrible memory.

One night we had a pizza party! Everyone piled into Mum's room, the boxes of pizza were delivered and we wheeled a television in so we could watch all the programmes we liked to watch at home. Before she was ill, we'd had a Saturday night tradition of watching *Challenge Anneka* and *The Generation Game* with a Domino's pizza. We made her time in the hospice really special. Writing this book is forcing me to think about those times from an adult perspective and I'm realising now how glad I am that I had such a limited understanding of her death – it made everything a lot easier.

After a few weeks, Mum's breathing changed. It had been getting steadily worse and she must have been in a coma but I was told she was asleep. The hospice contacted Dad, who whisked me out of school, saying we had to get to Mum RIGHT NOW. I remember how fast he drove and how alarmed I was. I don't remember visiting her and I don't remember saying goodbye. It kills me that I can't recall that moment, my last moment with her.

One night soon after, I stayed with Dad's parents, Peggy and John, my wonderful grandparents. I woke up very early the next morning and heard Dad come in and tell them Mum had died. She was 37. I lay in bed and thought, 'Well, that's that.' I faced the inevitable with all the pragmatism of a seven-year-old who doesn't have the first clue of what death actually means. Dad came up and sat on the edge of my bed, facing the wall. I know now what a terrible moment that must have been for him. 'Mummy has died,' he said, 'she's gone to be with the angels.' 'That's sad,' I said. I don't think either of us really knew what else to say. It was 20th December 1992.

That same day, we went to the funeral directors and picked out a headstone, one with a rose carved into it and the line 'Till We Meet Again'. The funeral was on 23rd December, a few days later, with the wake back at our house. It was just like a big party, full of all my favourite people, Mum would have loved it. I've since asked Dad how he managed to organise everything so quickly and he said, 'I had no choice, we had to do it before Christmas so that people could move on.' I love this about my dad – he's a doer even in the very depths of the worst things.

On Christmas Eve, I went to bed full of excitement that Father Christmas was on his way. I woke in the middle of the night to see Dad standing in my room with a stocking (well, a pillow case – is it just us that did that?) full of presents. Mandy in my class at school had told me Father Christmas wasn't real and I'd refused to believe her but had a niggling doubt. My dad was horrified that I had caught him and, even though I challenged him, he said he was just helping. I knew it, Father Christmas did not exist. This was turning out to be the worst Christmas ever. I had just recovered from a terrible stomach bug, my mother had died, we had buried her and now I knew there was no Santa. It doesn't get much worse than this. Oh wait, it does: read on.

The huge pile of presents I woke up to the following morning was a lovely distraction. It turns out you're given a LOT more gifts than usual when your mum has just died. I asked Dad when Mum was coming back to open hers and he explained again, ever so gently, that she lived with the angels now and that she wouldn't be coming home to open the presents with us. I feel so sorry for my dad that he had to keep explaining that to me, it must have been such a dagger through his heart every time he had to reiterate the news. It slowly dawned on me. My mum wasn't coming back, not even for Christmas.

By mid-morning, in her place instead was a strange woman I had never met before, a friend of Dad's who had popped in for a coffee on Christmas morning. It was now officially the worst week of my life.

A sort of normality returned. I am told I went to a counsellor but I don't remember it. My grandparents came every day to do the school run and be there every evening. My grandma was the loveliest sort, surrounding me with practical care and a big heart. She would drive me up to see my gran, who had made a folder of letters about my mum, people she had known who wrote about her so I would know what kind of person she was. Everyone did the very best they could and I am eternally grateful for their love because although there is a Mum-shaped hole in my heart, there are no scars at all.

# Chapter 3

# Single Mum Life

As an adult, I obviously missed having Mum in my life. I missed her dropping me off at uni, watching me graduate and meeting the people that mean a lot to me. I missed her every day but it wasn't until I became a mother myself though that I *really* missed her and then, add to that being a single mum, and we're really feeling it now. My mum was the one person I wanted to share the lows (many) and the highs (few) of the situation I now found myself in.

This had not been part of my happy-ever-after, fairytale life plan. How could I have been so stupid to let my future and, more importantly, the future of my daughter, suddenly look so unstable? The choice was simple – stay in a marriage that wasn't working for the sake of Darcy or break out into a brave new world, free to be a happy and loving parent to my little girl. Both were guaranteed to be hard on her for different reasons but she was still tiny and I figured I had a chance to change things for the better.

I know from the depths of my heart and soul that I made the right decision but the breakdown of my marriage is still my biggest life regret. I don't think I will ever feel good about it; there is no joy to be had from it. Not because I wish I was still in it, I am happier than I have ever been, but because of Darcy. I know it will have damaged her in some way; even though I truly believe it has caused less damage than us staying together, I will still beat myself up over it, worrying that I've hurt her. The thought of how my actions shaped her life makes my heart hurt and it has also defined my mothering of her. There is a small part of me that will always feel I am a single mum to Darcy, even though Liam would do anything for her and is the most brilliant stepfather (spoiler alert). I think it's because I know that ultimately the responsibility sits on my shoulders, I have the official and legal parental responsibility and the choices around her childhood lay with me. This is a blessing because that's exactly what she is, but since Liam's not her biological father, I do, very, very deep down, feel a bit alone.

Single motherhood is Motherhood Plus or Motherhood X 10 and the early days were bloody hard. There was no plan to follow, it was like turning up on a strange island without a map, the right currency or a phone charger. It was a step-by-step process, getting through each day and night, putting space between now and the old life as we headed into a new era. We had to find our routine. Parenting is designed to be done in partnership and suddenly, I was either totally responsible for half the week or without my child for the other half. Just because I didn't have Darcy full-time didn't mean I wasn't a complete mother or that I could switch off the love and care when I was without her.

Even though I knew it was good for her to have a life with her dad and that she loved him dearly, I dreaded Darcy leaving me. Until you have been in that situation you cannot imagine how tough it can be and I speak as someone who has a hands-on ex-husband. There are many women who are single parents all the time and valiantly being both mum and dad. I have complete, utmost and eternal respect for them. They are absolute goddesses in my book.

I never thought I would feel this but I did: I felt so, so ashamed of myself. I had a failed marriage (I should say again now, for no big scandalous reason. Neither of us had an affair or were awful, we just grew up and grew apart), a daughter who was the product of a broken family and I felt exposed, vulnerable and embarrassed. There was now a new car on the driveaway. How long before the neighbours noticed the car we used to share was gone and I'd bought my own and started to speculate? I had to let Darcy's nursery know that she now had two addresses. I had to change my banking. I had to put just my name on the bills. I had to know what day the bins go out. I had let the side down even though I wasn't even sure what or where the side was!

When we are little we play Mums and Dads, we don't play Single Mummies Weeping Silently in the Bath With a Baileys Whilst Netflix Plays Something Gentle Because You Can't Handle Anything But Reruns of *Friends*. Modern society (or at least the skewed version I saw every day on Instagram) seems to favour the nuclear family – the unit of mum, dad and two beautiful children in Joules raincoats. Add a photogenic puppy, a Starbucks coffee cup and a family trip to somewhere with a good sun flair photo op and you've absolutely WON life. I wasn't managing any of that.

Every so often, I see how far we have come, accepting blended families, same-sex couples, fostering and adoption arrangements, but it's still not far enough. I still felt like people judged me as a single mum. One day, not long after I became one, I was in Morrisons doing a shop. I stood in the chilled aisle holding a family-size carton of orange juice and I just cried. Big, massive, heaving tears by the way, not a dainty tear falling quietly down my cheek. I stood there looking at that massive 'family size' carton of orange juice and thought, 'I can't buy this, I'm not in a family anymore.' That was a low day. There were a lot of those.

I have experienced all sorts of versions of loneliness in my life but being a single mum was in a league of its own. There was the type of lonely that hit me when my little girl was at her dad's house and how empty my place would feel. I would always send her off with positive chat about how much fun she would have and how I couldn't wait to hear all about it. When she left, I tried avoiding her room, not going in when she wasn't there, but that felt worse, like I was fully closing a piece of my heart, so I left her door open and popped in and out with the hoover and piles of clean washing and occasionally I sat on her bed for a moment, just to feel nearer to her. When she came home, I made a conscious decision not to tell her how much I missed her because I didn't want her to feel any guilt or sadness for being away. I'd ask her if she'd had a lovely time, squeeze her tight and say a silent 'Thank you' that she was back.

There was another type of loneliness when Darcy was with me, though. See? It's very hard to win the Single Mum game – not impossible but definitely hard. When she was home, the responsibility to keep her safe, fed, happy and entertained was enormous. The pressure built when both of us were tired, grumpy and whingy but I didn't have somebody else I could share that with. There was nobody to discuss the everyday, little things with, nobody to do one thing (like clear the kitchen up from dinner), while the other did another (like bathtime) – you just have to do it all yourself. There's nobody to help put the buggy and bags in the boot while you lift the kiddo into the car and grapple about with the car seat harness – you just have to do it all yourself. I could go on and on about all the things you have to do yourself. You suddenly realise how much easier life is in a pair than alone.

I'll never forget the spring morning I woke up to a skip outside my house. I'd ordered it weeks prior, when I knew I had a free weekend, because I was going to have a huge clear out of my whole house. I'd bought new garden furniture and I'd decluttered everywhere. Except, the garden furniture had come flatpack and I didn't know how to build it; the piles of things I'd made for the skip/recycling/charity shops were so heavy I was struggling to take them anywhere and I just felt like I was drowning in my own life.

Well, this is where friends come in. My wonderful, fabulous friends Mark and Clare came over and saved the day! Mark built my flatpack picnic table, Clare helped me move my piles of stuff, I had a good cry and cuddle of their then new baby

Hope and by bedtime that night my house was an oasis of calm and order. We did it! Not in the conventional family way, but we still did it!* Over the next few years, I spent a lot of time making my home really cosy and lovely for Darcy and me, imagining us there for years.

As well as being physically draining, single parenthood was a lot more isolating than I expected. I was either the single mum with child looking for someone we could arrange a playdate with or I was on my own. It wasn't too bad during the week but at the weekend, all my friends had family time or days out with their children and husbands. They'd invite me to come along but spending a day with (what I felt like was) a perfect family didn't appeal.

So I found lots of things for Darcy and me to do alone. It forced me to be more sociable and open to new friendships than I would otherwise have been. I accepted play dates, was proactive about messaging mums and suggesting park meet ups or inviting everyone over for a natter and fish fingers. Turned out, it was good for me! A sisterhood of mums, if you will. A gang of maternal

---

* Little spoiler – Clare has now had a second baby, just after I had my second baby (told you this is a spoiler) and we are still close friends, supporting and loving. Mum Friends are truly the best.

huggers. The thing about mums is that most of them are mums to everyone. They are little mums to each other, offering a shoulder to cry on, a bag of chocolate buttons, a sounding board and a big laugh. We had each other's backs and each other's hearts and I started to feel a bit better.

Family was also invaluable. My Aunty Judith would fill my fridge with homemade meals in Tupperware pots. She made me the sort of dishes I loved as a child, like her sweet potato korma or Granny's 'homity pie'. I felt completely loved and cared for by her. Sometimes I would come home from a long work day in London and there would be a lemon drizzle cake in the porch with a note from her saying 'Love you lots'. I'd pick up the cake, unlock my front door, have a little cry and be so glad for that slice of flipping cake. Now she comes to me almost every Tuesday and I look after her – we call it Ju'sDay Tuesday. I cook dinner for her and she and the children pretend it's really nice, even though we all know that my food is pretty dire. The other week I made her a five-bean chilli and she said it was the best five-bean chilli she had ever had on a Tuesday . . . You can tell she's a mum too!

As a single mum I was constantly questioning my parenting. Not so that Darcy picked up on it or sensed my fear or hesitation, but I was always aware of how I was managing. The spotlight was now fully on me and I couldn't step out of it. I didn't want to be that parent who was too tired to uphold boundaries and let bedtime slip, or who didn't cook proper dinners (as proper as I do anyway, haha!) or who wasn't firm just so I didn't have to be 'bad cop'. I didn't want to be in a competition with her dad about who loved her most and I didn't want to be too busy with all the other things life was throwing at me to not be Fun Mummy.

Motherhood is all about balance and in those early days I didn't have anyone close I could discuss this with. In reality, I probably could have but I felt so ashamed of what I perceived as my shortcomings that I just kept it all in. I fantasised about how lovely it would have been to have my own mum there to help me. I'd have loved to have given her a call to tell her about our day or to arrange something fun at the weekend. What I wanted was somebody at the end of the day to say, 'Well done, you have done enough, it's all going to be OK,' and give me a high five or a little air hug (you know I'm not a physical touch kind of a gal!). Not to congratulate or validate me, just to stand beside me, to have someone on my team.

There were two saving graces in those early days. The first was that I was in the fortunate position of having a financial safety net. I had built my business to a good point so money wasn't a huge barrier to a new independent life. I know how lucky I am. I have friends who have really struggled, stuck in relationships they don't want to be in but without the funds to leave or end it. Money holds people together at those times when they should be walking away and starting afresh.

Being a single mum with one salary to rely on forced me to make wise money choices and I like to think this hasn't changed. I'm the kind of person who always has a plan A, B, C and D so I have emergency pots and procedures in place to make sure we'll be OK, whatever's around the corner. Liam and I are so happy together and I'd like to think that will never ever change, but if life's taught me anything so far, it's that things don't always go to plan and it doesn't hurt to be prepared. Now if that's not the most romantic thing I've ever said, I don't know what is, haha!

My second (and biggest) saving grace was Darcy. She was an absolute delight, the light of my life, the apple of my eye, and made the whole single parent gig as easy as it could have been. I have talked about her throughout the book but it doesn't hurt to repeat how immensely, heartfillingly proud I am of her. Right from the start, I could see she was an old soul, very loving, very empathetic, and she moved through each stage of her early life without being too fazed.

Our time together as a twosome was very special. Partly because I only had her for half the week and also because I knew (well, I hoped) one day it may be more than just her and me together at home. I would organise lots of fun things for her – fish finger parties with friends, days out joining me for work things in London where I'd add on something fun like the Rainforest Café or a mooch round the big Lush on Oxford Street. I also flew us out a few times to Seattle to visit my wonderful friend Marie and her family. Spending time with Darcy is a hoot, she has always been great company, but just to balance out the smoosh, here are a few examples of when things haven't been quite so fairytale . . .

I had taken Darcy out for a breakfast treat; she was only four or five. We would occasionally go out together to eat, particularly brunch or lunch, which is much easier than taking a small child out for dinner. Darcy and I both love doing this and I have been taking her out from when she was quite little. It doesn't have to be an expensive treat, just the opportunity to sit opposite each other and chat without me having to cook and clear up. Bliss. There was a tearoom we were usually keen on but I decided to take Darcy somewhere new as a bit of a change. We sat down, only one other table was occupied, and we gave our order to a lovely lady. She was very welcoming, commenting on how she had not seen us before and how great it was to have us there for the first time. The room was unnervingly quiet. Darcy took a bite of her breakfast and I asked her encouragingly if it was delicious. 'It's not as good as the other place we go to, Mummy, their breakfast is better,' she said loudly. The woman looked at me and I looked at her and prayed for the ground to swallow me up immediately. At least she knows what she likes!

There was also the time I took Darcy to America with me to see lovely Marie. While we were there, I tried to take Darcy to as many things as possible. So, we went out shopping and Darcy wanted to buy some little gifts to take home with her for family and friends. We popped into a bookshop, which turned out to be a Christian bookstore, run by a lovely, chatty lady. Darcy found something she wanted to buy for her grandad so I gave her the money and she went to the till confidently, me just behind her. I was quite proud of how able she felt to handle the transaction. Anyway, the lady, a devout Christian with a cross round her neck and a pile of Bibles next to her, asked Darcy her name and how old she was. Darcy said in a big voice, 'My name is Darcy and I am five years old but my mummy makes me say four when we go on the train so she doesn't have to pay for a ticket.' God forgive me! (Also, it was ONE time!)

Out of the mouths of babes, eh?!

Being a single mum was a game changer. I think I felt grown-up way before my time. I blame my lost childhood for that. I thought I was a grown-up when I left home and lived with my uni girlfriends but when I locked the front door at night, of the home I now owned all by myself, Darcy tucked up in bed, just me, her and the cats, I realised that this was being adult. The responsibility felt huge. It was what I had chosen and I also knew how much it would take out of me. If this is you now, don't despair. You can absolutely do this! I'm no stronger or bolder than you. If I can do it, so can you! You can smash it, in fact! When things are tough, take a little look at the list I have included here. I hope it helps in some way.

## Self-Care for Single Mums

1. *Loneliness – don't underestimate this emotion. It can floor you regularly without warning. Also know that you can be just as lonely in a bad relationship as you can be out of it, so that is not a reason to stick with it. Feel the feels, talk openly about them and find things and people who lift you.*

2. The lasting effect on my child – I can't tell you how Darcy will turn out. Of course, I desperately hope she'll be happy and healthy for all of her days. She is currently nine and a happy, loving and open person. She doesn't appear to be scarred by the experience or the way her life has changed but I won't know this until she is emotionally mature enough to tell me if I have totally screwed her up and whether she needs therapy. I am not saying this flippantly, I really don't know what she will think. You just have to do what you think is for the best at the time you are doing it. Bit of a blind faith thing, I guess.

3. Self-doubt – is normal but do not let it rule you. We all suffer with this and it is particularly shouty and in your face as a single parent. It is good to question your actions and motives but, at some point, you have to make the decision, take the responsibility and trust that you are right. When Darcy was little those choices were about small things but, as she grows, so will the size and importance of those things. You have to pull your big girl pants up (full cotton briefs for me, please), take a breath and trust that you're making the best decision you can right now with the information

and knowledge you have. I'm giving you a big encouraging fist pump across the pages! Come on!

4. Custody arrangements – whatever you are dealing with, whether it is shifting boundaries, absence or dominance, put your child first. I don't know a single person who found this process easy and smooth because it is a negotiation between two people who love their child more than anything but perhaps don't love (or even like) each other a whole lot. You feel like you have everything at stake with the one person you don't want any kind of relationship with, but here you are, trying to arrange the most important thing in the world to you. I know this is boring and I know this is hard but every possible chance you can – take the high road. Michelle Obama said, 'When they go low, we go high.' Say this to yourself every time the phone pings, the solicitor letter pops through the door or your emails buzz regarding custody. One day your baby will grow up and thank you for it.

5. Cut yourself some slack – this also appears on the surviving motherhood list and I had to be stopped repeating it everywhere I could. You are doing your best.

Relax, lower your standards a little, aim for happiness and acceptance between you and your child. I started this single-parent journey expecting to be one sort of mother. The sort that wears clean navy and white striped Breton tops. It turns out I have been something quite different and perfect isn't possible. Reaching the end of the day having had a shower, however, is possible. Hurrah for that. Celebrate the small wins.

6. Love who you become – I changed so much as a single mum. It is not an experience I would have chosen but it is one of those things that makes you stronger. I've toughened up in all the good ways, I think. I know that if I had to face it again, I could. In fact, there ended up being big parts of it that I loved, and if Liam wasn't reading this book (!) I'd say there were little parts of it that I miss. I think being a single parent offers you an opportunity to learn life skills you never thought you'd need and that's something to be grateful for. If I may be so bold (I think I probably can since this is my own book and if you're not going to toot your own horn on your own pages, where are you, eh?), I think I've become a better person for it. Four for me! (Name that reference, teehee!)

7. The ex – if you feel any kind of negativity towards your ex, shield your child from it. Keep the disagreements between adults and don't put the children in the middle of it. They are more aware of conflict than you think. If you don't have anything nice to say, just keep things neutral. Neutral is fine. The more you behave neutrally about things, the more you'll actually feel neutral. Nobody wants to walk through life feeling angry and sad and frustrated so I think this is actually a pretty good side effect of being a good mummy!

8. (I realise this is going to sound contradictory to my last point but let's go with it.) Honest emotion – Darcy was very aware of my moods and would pick up on when I was feeling low and ask me if I was sad. At first I brushed it off and would say I was fine, but I could tell that left her feeling confused and doubting her abilities to read things. I think it helped both of us for me to be honest and say, 'Yes, I was feeling a little sad but not for long and it wasn't anybody's fault.' I wanted to validate her intuitive reaction but not worry her. Encouraging your child to talk about things and properly listening to them is fundamental, whatever situation you are in. The caveat I would add here is

not to discuss money with them if they are still quite young – the lack of it and the anxiety you may have around it. Find another adult for those chats.

9. Talk it out – make those connections with other mums that I mentioned earlier in the chapter. A girl gang around you really helps and having other children around to play with yours creates a sociable normal. You may also have a family member you respect and trust and can go to for advice.

10. Be organised – I missed Darcy desperately so I had to have a plan when I was on my own. I really learnt to make the most of my time and scheduled as much of my work stuff into my days without her as I could. I also treated myself to long hot baths and . . . ooh-er . . . dated. More on that in a mo!

11. Routine – is crucial for all of you, particularly the child in the middle. Knowing when they are going to be at which parent's house and making that transition as easy as possible is your parental responsibility. Don't make them feel guilty for having fun when they are not with you and don't gush and fawn over them when they return (though honestly, every time

Darcy came home I nearly squished her to pieces). If you behave as if this arrangement is normal then it will help your child accept it too.

12. Family – OK, it looks different, it's not what you dreamt of, but by now we know life isn't a fairytale. Things happen and it doesn't mean you have failed. Look at it from a different perspective and count your blessings. Don't forget friends are often closer than family and you can actually choose them – woo!

13. Your nest – create a cosy environment, a sanctuary for you and your child. Make it a home, whether it is two of you or six. It should be the safest place for you all to be and connect. Feather that nest, my friend! A cosy home is a happy home if you ask me!

14. No judgement – walk away from those who try to judge you or make you feel worse than you already do. Beware of those who are smug about their own lives in the face of yours falling apart. Though you do not know what goes on in each home and what may lie behind the perfect family façade. You are just as valid and worthy as anyone else on this earth. Stand tall.

15. Take a break – I know, I say this a lot, but as a single parent it is imperative and yet often impossible. Suggest a child swap with a friend for an afternoon. Have their children one week and they have yours the next. Brief respite can be enough to rebuild you.

16. Find a good soft play – this is your best friend so don't slate it. The children can play, you can have a coffee, chat to a friend, read a magazine, look at your social media, everyone is happy. Who needs a boyfriend when there's a ball pool?

17. TV for all – let them watch some during the day when you need to have a break. I've looked into the science of it and it turns out their eyes won't actually physically turn square. Phew! Then, when they are in bed, do not underestimate the power of a gentle box set on Netflix. I can binge-watch period dramas, comedy and romance and feel better instantly.

18. Give yourself permission to move on. You deserve joy. Moving on might not be a new partner. It might be just allowing yourself to smile again. *insert little heart emoji from me to you right here*

# Chapter 4

## The Dating Game: You've Got to Kiss a Lot of Frogs

So where was I? Oh yes, single and not wanting to mingle. Darcy was the main thing that kept me going, made me jump(ish) out of bed in the morning, face the day and get sh*t done. It was character building. That's what we say when we can't think of anything positive about a situation; we call it character building, don't we?

I made an effort to make more friends. I forced myself to talk to other mums in the school playground and invited them over for play dates and kids' tea parties. One of those new friends, Esther, became a best friend, which was such a gift for me – to this day she's an utter blessing. Gradually I could see the joy in my new life and, confident that Darcy was happy, safe and well when she wasn't with me, I started to enjoy my alone time. I had three days a week and I used them wisely. I didn't want to sit on the sofa every night pining for Darcy so I started to go out. I tentatively hit the dating scene.

My dating history has been an interesting series of mishaps, broken hearts, hilarity and weirdness, some of which I have shared on my YouTube channel (anyone remember the Lizard Man?) and some of which I have kept to myself. Until now. Dun dun duuunnn. It feels like the right place and the right time to tell these stories, particularly as most of my dating happened when I was a single mum and this is, after all, all about the #MumLife.

I had very few dates before I met and married Darcy's dad. I arrived at university naive and low on confidence but ready for any exciting dalliance that might come my way. It was a lethal combination. I embraced the student socials, thrilled to be part of the cool, edgy nightlife of Liverpool's Concert Square.

One night I met an attractive American guy in his thirties, propping up the bar, oozing maturity and sophistication from every cleansed pore. He told me he owned a radio station and a house on the Cayman Islands. I know what you are thinking and you are probably right. He may well have been a fantasist but he bought me and my friends a round of drinks and 18-year-old Louise was impressed – it didn't take much. I wasn't going to get that sort of attention from a fellow student, this was a real man who would treat me properly, I thought, entirely based on one free Southern Comfort and lemonade. I didn't hesitate to say yes to a date. I was 18 and I was finally going to have a proper boyfriend! That's exactly what this meant, 100 per cent!

We met for a drink. I had chosen an outfit that I felt was appropriate for the girlfriend of a businessman. A pink shirt, green jeans and pointy pink flats. I looked more like a hydrangea. Why not one friend said, 'burn those jeans and we'll never speak of them again,' I do not know. So there I was, clip-clopping across the cobbles like a mismatched plant, full of optimism and misplaced confidence.

I ignored all the usual rules and went back to his apartment (sorry, Dad), a duplex overlooking Concert Square. It was incredibly cool. He put a film on the projector – that's how damn cool it all was, there was a projector. Fancy. He poured me red wine (fancy again), which I didn't like but drank anyway. This was beyond what I had expected from my first boyfriend. He hadn't actually said he was my boyfriend, but I didn't know how dating worked so presumed we were an item now. I was beside myself. As the evening progressed, he said he would give me a tour of his place, which was odd because his apartment was open-plan and I could see everything from the sofa. All except the bedroom. He gave me a detailed commentary on his surroundings as we walked around and then found ourselves standing by his big bed.

'This is my bed,' he said, pointing at his bed, me nodding. There was a long pause and he gave me a lingering look. 'I am definitely not ready for this,' I thought. Naively, this is not where I had expected the evening to go. He walked over to his bedside table and pulled open the drawer. Oh, what could be in here? Sophisticated books? His collection of expensive watches? Condoms? Nope. It was crammed full of wrapped tampons. All the colours for all your flows.

'If you ever need anything,' he said breezily, gesturing to the drawer before he closed it. 'I'm OK for now, thank you,' I stuttered. It was the weirdest thing. He didn't acknowledge that it was a bit unusual for a single, 30-something man to have a drawer full (and I mean full, like at least 70–100 in there, floating around like sweets in a Christmas tin, not in the boxes) of feminine hygiene products. What did he think I was going to do? Grab a few for my handbag and thank him? I thought it might be best to leave my new boyfriend who wasn't my boyfriend.

He walked me home. Outside my student halls, we stopped awkwardly, he leant in for a kiss. I put my hand on his shoulder and said, 'Bless you,' like a panicked nun and ran inside. I never saw him again. He didn't call me and I didn't call him. I also never wore the green jeans again either. Both things were probably for the best but I am sad

I missed out on the free tamps. You win some, you lose some, eh?

As my marriage came to an end, I knew I would be back out on the dating scene eventually. I had little experience of dating before marriage and I was about to go back out there, though this time as a single parent with a young child who was my absolute priority. It took me a while to be ready to date. I thought, 'Hey, once everyone knows I am single all those boys who have always fancied me will just get in touch, right?' I won't have to sign up for a dating app or hang out in a bar because these boys have been waiting for me, pining, and they'll be all like, 'Wow, Louise, you're available, let's go out.'

Nobody rang. Nobody text. Nobody slid into anything, let alone my DMs.

I gave them a little helping hand by posting a status on Facebook that went a bit like this: 'Yes, it's true, I am now single. If anybody is harbouring any feelings for me please do feel free to get in touch. Send me a DM if you are too shy to write . . .'

Nothing. Not a sausage. Not a single person had been secretly harbouring any feelings of love or lust for me. This was going to be tougher than I had first thought.

Then a breakthrough. A male friend of mine texted me: *Hey! I would love to take you out for dinner and a chat if you're free!*

'Oh, would you now?' I thought, realising he had always had a soft spot for me. This was it, my friends, I was back on the scene!

I jollied myself up (green skirt, black top, cute pumps), told my friends I was off on a date and met him for a romantic walk by the river and dinner in a lovely Italian restaurant. *Très* romantic, *non*?

When home, I texted him: *Thanks for a lovely dinner and evening, I had a great time. x*

I guessed (after about 45 minutes of mental debate) one kiss was OK, as none looked too formal and two was too many. He immediately responded (he couldn't get enough of me, obviously!). *Thanks for being such great company! X* Woo! A kiss in return!

The following day, he messaged to suggest a spa trip after we had both been talking about how much we loved a pamper. As second dates go this was ambitious, but who was I to complain? A romantic spa trip is never going to be a no from me. He suggested we invite a mutual friend and her boyfriend along too. I responded with, *Yes, but wouldn't it be more romantic if it was just the two of us?*

Immediately my phone started flashing. He was calling me! Who makes actual phone calls these days? I knew I couldn't ignore it because I'd literally just text so he'd know I had my phone in my hand, but also, A PHONE CALL? HELP!

He was just ringing, he said, because he was worried I had misunderstood the tone of his text. He didn't see this as a romantic thing, just friends hanging out, and wasn't that how I felt too? Weren't we just chilling out together? Just 'hanging'? Just grabbing dinner and bants here and there?

'YES,' I squeaked, in a voice so high it could only be heard by field mice. Totally, that is completely me, I AM SO CHILL. Just sat here chilling, wanting to JUST HANG WITH MY FRIENDS. Laughing conspiratorially and claiming it was all for the bants, I put the phone down. I wanted to crawl into a hole, rip my own face off and eat it. What a jolly good start.

My next foray into dating was no better. A friend of mine decided to set me up with her brother. He had also been through a break-up and was a single parent. This was a huge relief as I thought he would understand how Darcy would always be first in my life. Plus, he worked in the City, which sounded financially sensible. I base that on absolutely nothing other than 'the City' sounds quite upmarket, doesn't it?

I combined our lunch date with a few days of London work, arriving to meet him in a restaurant a little flustered with an overly large suitcase. 'Hello,' I said, 'I hope this date goes well because I'm staying at your house,' I joked, silently praising myself for an excellent ice breaker. 'I'm not sure I am ready for that sort of thing,' he replied, deadpan. No sense of humour, clearly.

It didn't get any better. I ordered pesto pasta (honestly, cut me open and I'd bleed pesto, I love it that much) and when it arrived, he looked at it disdainfully and asked if I had ordered it from the children's menu. So, he wasn't funny and he was a food shamer, great. He had the goat curry. Which he then continued to offer me tasters of despite my saying I was a vegetarian four whole times. When I told him I was writing a book he gave me a patronising little smile and said, 'Well, it's good to keep yourself occupied.' This was my second dating attempt and it was as disastrous as the first. While we're here, in case Mr Goat Curry is reading this, that book you were so patronising of, well, it turned out to be a *Sunday Times* number one bestseller and has been translated into numerous languages and sold all around the world. It *was* good to keep myself occupied after all, eh?

Back to dating. Why couldn't I find the right guy? What was wrong with me? I asked a good male friend that question in the hope he'd be able to banish my fears and give me a bit of reassurance. He answered worryingly quickly, 'I often ask myself what it is about you that I don't find attractive.'

Often. How bloody often do you consider this? 'Thanks very much,' I said, 'that really helps.'

Another male pal once told me, 'If you were two stone lighter then I think I probably could. . .' What a champ of a man. For the record, even if I were two stone lighter, I never would. Ha! (I've said it in a book now, so I've had the last chubby laugh, haven't I?) I did have a little secret cry over that one though. I might be fat-skinned but I'm not that thick-skinned.

My saving grace, as usual, was my daughter. I wasn't looking for a man to marry or a replacement father figure for Darcy. I didn't want anyone to jeopardise my time with her, or for someone to move into our little home or try to co-parent with me. I just wanted some fun. With somebody I fancied, who fancied me. Was that so hard? I knew I was lucky – I had a gorgeous child, great friends and my career was flying.

I went off to a work conference in America at the tail end of 2014 and there I met Brad, a digital media colleague. (That's not his real name but you have to change these things for the legal eagles. We're still friends now – amazingly – and he'd actually be thrilled I've included him in a book!) He was six foot three with dark, Jon Snow-esque hair and handsome with a brilliant white smile. After a panel discussion we were on together, he invited me and my friends to a party later that evening. Maybe this was it? I stopped myself doodling my name with his surname.

At the party, my friends made me look cool by surrounding me with adoration and pretending to laugh heartily at all my jokes (I wish I was that funny that they were really laughing but alas, I'm at least grateful for the favour!). It worked and Brad hung out with us all evening. We became friends. That was it though, nothing romantic, despite having little butterflies in my tummy every time he so much as looked at me. I headed back to the UK, left my butterflies stateside, and we kept in vague contact but I wasn't in the right head space to pursue anything.

Several months later, we bumped into each other at another conference in the States. We hung out together, talking in hotel bars into the early hours, learning more and more about each other. As a joke, I asked him what he was doing the following month. 'Why don't you come to the UK?' I said and he said, 'Why not?' I took his diary and wrote across the agreed week:

*Falling in love with Louise Pentland*

It was a joke. Come on now, of course it was just a joke . . . When he rang me a few weeks later and told me he was in Paris, I said I was in London and to hop on the Eurostar. He did! The man literally travelled across a country to spend time with me! This in itself felt like a win.

Brad arrived the day I was booked to interview Ed Miliband. Before the interview, I dashed to St Pancras to meet him. Someone was playing the piano on the station concourse as he stepped off the train, all tall and excitingly American, and it felt like we were in a movie. I just had to sort out a quick Ed Miliband interview first and then I could casually fall wildly in love.

We went straight to YouTube HQ and I confess I interviewed Ed with my head still half in the lobby, where Brad sat waiting patiently. We had an amazing night together with friends at a very swish restaurant called Sketch (me and Brad, not Ed, although he would have been very welcome to join us) and I fell head over heels for him. He ordered me a cocktail – 'I know you will love it' – and inside I swooned.

He was kind, capable and attentive. A man who shared and understood my work environment, who appreciated me, who wasn't going to compromise my home life. I thought he was completely and utterly the bee's knees. I was besotted. I took my courage in my hands and asked him what this was, what we were. I was sure he felt the same.

'Just friends,' he said. 'For now.'

I'll just let that sink in for a mo. Took me about a week, but you have about a nanosecond because the next paragraph needs to be read.

I was booked for a work event in New York which coincided with my thirtieth birthday. It sounds spoilt to say this, but it wasn't where I wanted to be celebrating a new decade. I wanted to be at home with Darcy and my friends around me. I couldn't miss this annual summit, it was the big date of the YouTube calendar, but I wished it hadn't clashed. I was cheered by the knowledge that I would see Brad again, even though he had been clear ('for now') about our relationship status. We had been video calling and messaging each other every day since the last meeting though so that seemed promising.

I arrived in NYC and stepped into the most incredible week of my life. The lovely people at YouTube surprised me the day before my birthday with a sparkly pink cake at an event and David Blaine (who had been booked for the event) taught me magic tricks on stage. Brad was there and said he was taking me out for a birthday surprise. He knew my geek interest in railways (don't judge me, I'm really into transport, OK?!) and had hired a bar decked out like a train carriage for me and my YouTube pals to celebrate in. They had created a special 'Louise' cocktail and Brad had put together a photobook of our time in London together. I was a complete mess. This man had gone to so much effort to please me, to wow me. This man, who was just a friend, had given me a book full of pictures of us TOGETHER. He announced he had another surprise for me.

We went for a walk through Manhattan at night. I started to feel the cold in my cocktail dress so he sent me back up to my hotel room to find something warm to wear. I hadn't packed for a moonlit walk through the city. All I had was a hoodie. Which wouldn't have been quite so bad but across my tits it said, 'Cats are my thing', except instead of 'my' it read 'meow'. So I was now wearing a hoodie that was too tight for me, with 'Cats are meow thing' strained across my sausage boob. I would have been better off coming out in the hotel duvet.

We walked to the Empire State Building. Brad had tickets and we zoomed up to the top just in time for midnight. As I stepped into a new decade, he looked me in the eyes and, in his sexy drawl, said, 'Happy birthday, Louise, would you like your present now?'

'This. Is. It. This. Is. The. Moment,' I thought. 'He is 100 per cent going to kiss me. I don't care if I am wearing a tight cat hoodie over a cocktail dress, this is what I have been waiting for!' I lifted my face and . . . he pulled out ear pods and put them in my ears.

He had recorded himself singing Estelle's 'American Boy' a cappella, renaming it 'American Boy Pentland', changing the lyrics to incorporate our in-jokes and references to me. It must have taken him hours or days to write and record this. It was one of the most amazing, romantic things anyone has ever done for me. It was incredible, but, surely to God, now we should kiss? I thought, 'To hell with this! I'm 30. I'm confident! I'm saying it!' I suggest a small smooch. 'No,' he said, 'this isn't the time.' We walked back to my hotel. If this wasn't the time then it wasn't going to be any time. The perfect night, the most romantic date and we were still just friends. I was beyond confused. Maybe it was the cat hoodie?

The next day, we went to a baseball match together, another PR work event with friends, but Brad and I sat next to each other. There was a party in the evening at Madison Square Garden and Snoop Dogg was DJ'ing. I promise you, I am not making this up, it really was just a mind-blowing trip! Brad and I went together but I lost him at the party and he didn't make an effort to find me, despite my messaging him several times, which was another warning sign I chose to ignore. I was annoyed but he'd given me so much of his time the other nights back at the hotel – again, never anything sexual, just sitting talking all freaking night. This man was a dream really.

The following morning, he messaged me to say he would see me before my flight. I thought he meant he was coming to the airport before I headed home. What he actually meant was that he had booked a car to pick me up and take me to a helipad, where we were taking off for a helicopter ride around

Manhattan... (I haven't even mentioned the spa treatment he booked for me. I mean, tell me, what is a girl to think?!)

I asked him outright. It was all amazing, everything he had done, I felt completely spoilt and loved and yet . . . 'Just friends,' he repeated, 'that could become something else one day.' Right now it was work-related, a bit of good schmoozing from him and making me feel at home in the city. Really? A photobook? The 'Louise' cocktails in the train carriage bar? Coming to my hotel room and talking all night? Recording a personalised song? That's not just 'networking', surely? Maybe I've been doing it all wrong!

I went home in love (and bewildered). He followed me to the UK the next month, met my family (not Darcy), came to my local pub and handwrote my dad a letter after meeting him. Then I went to Los Angeles and Brad took me out on a boat. Yes, he sailed and had hired a boat. I know, the guy is unreal. Can I remind you, as I continued to remind myself, we were still JUST FRIENDS. Except, in his hometown the cracks started to show. He didn't invite me to his apartment even once, he disappeared at random times and there were last-minute work meetings really late at night. I will leave you to come to your own conclusions here.

My friends were sick of hearing about Brad. They knew, long before I did, that it was never going to be what I wanted it to be. I was addicted to someone I had no physical relationship with, who kept me at arm's length and was then wildly, unpredictably romantic. He and I did talk about the future, the futility of being in different countries, neither of us willing to up sticks and move. Darcy came first. There was no way I could leave England.

Throughout this time I continued to date. I wasn't in a relationship, I was in an infatuation and I needed real-life scenarios to ground me. The problem was that nothing compared to the whirlwind excitement of the Beautiful American and our champagne and macaroni cheese suppers (I could fill a whole book just with the Brad romance but I know he'll read this and I know he'll love it too much).

I downloaded Tinder. Here we go, eligible bachelors looking for a good time with nice, available women. What could go wrong here? These people had downloaded the app because they wanted more than 'just friends'. Surely this was the place for me?

My first match was John, a data analyst. He had put up a few wacky photos – one of him dressed as SuperTed, one of him in the pub with his mates and one black-and-white one of him skiing. He must be a fun guy, I thought, confident in his own skin if he is happy to post those sorts of pictures. I should note now, I soon discovered that almost all men on Tinder post the same pictures – mirror selfie fresh from the gym; black and white of them doing a sport (usually skiing); mates in pub; a 'fun' fancy dress and sometimes, if you're lucky, one with a dog in. It's like they get a little rule book when they sign up to the app that tells them, 'Women love these – don't forget to make the ski one black and white, though!' Sorry, I've gone off-piste. #Punny

We met in a pub and I knew immediately it was doomed. He was wearing combat trousers with zips at the knees so he could transform them speedily into shorts. It's a look that doesn't work for me. I'm not really sure who those shorts *do* work for actually. He also revealed he had been on Tinder for four years without success. 'Oh no! You poor thing,' I said sympathetically. Knowing how hard I'd found dating so far, I understood he must be struggling too. 'What went wrong?' I asked, softly joking. 'Well, I did meet someone but she was a single mum,' he replied. 'What a mess!' Surreptitiously, I sent my friend Clare a blank text, the signal we'd agreed beforehand, a rescue flare. She called me straight away and I put on my best surprised-my-phone-was-ringing face . . .

'Hi Clare, I can't really speak right now. What? My house? You drove past and the windows were smashed? Are you telling me that there has been a burglary at my house, Clare, and I need to come straight home?! Yes, of course, I am coming home now.'

Do feel free to employ this technique if you are ever stuck in a similar situation. You're welcome. I went home and face-timed Brad. My good FRIEND Brad.

The following week I attempted my second Tinder date. On meeting, he said, 'Louise, great name, it rhymes with cheese! Do a lot of people call you Cheese?' No, they don't. Nobody has ever called me Cheese. He asked if he could and I said, 'Oh haha, you can call me Louise or Lou.' He paid no attention to this and said, 'Come on, Cheesy, let's sit down.' We sat by the fire (actually, I sat a bit too close and nearly melted, but you know what it's like when you're too polite to say anything so you just grin and bear it) in a country pub. I knew we were struggling for common ground when he asked if I had any pets. 'Yes,' I said and before I could continue he laughed, 'Oh God, tell me you're not one of those crazy cat ladies?' Good job he'd never seen my super-cool cat hoodie, eh?

I played down how much I love cats and asked if he had any pets (wild conversation). 'Right, well, I have bearded dragons, two that I thought were both male, but one morning I came downstairs and there were 20 lizard eggs.' He had caught my interest. You don't very often hear about 20 surprise lizard eggs, do you? 'So, do you now have 22 bearded dragons?' I asked. 'No,' he said, 'I killed them. I froze the eggs and then I put them in the bin.' Silence. I felt a bit sick. I thought, why didn't he give them to a pet shop? A reptile sanctuary? If this man was capable of mass lizard murder, what else was he capable of? Then he said, 'The next time it happened I did feel a bit guilty though.' I made an excuse and went home.

Tell me if I am oversharing. I feel like I am on a bit of a roll. The more hilarious dating stories I remember the more I want to include them. Tinder was a wealth of brilliantly character-building experiences. Remember how if something isn't as great as you thought it would be it's just 'character building'? You can make anything better in your mind if you think of it like that . . .

One of my most hilarious experiences was a second date after the first one had been OK. It wasn't earth-shattering and Brad was still lurking in my long-distance life, but it was worth another go. To be quite honest with you, I was just amazed that we'd reached Date #2. We decided to go for a picnic by the river, watch the sunset, drink and chat. It was going fairly well until I needed a wee. Normally, I have a bladder the size of Lake Victoria, but that evening I was desperate to go, there was no way out of it. I will say though, I'm not a girl who can usually wee outside and I wasn't comfortable telling him anything to do with my toileting, so I sat in severe pain for a while, convinced my bladder would explode. That would be better. A full-on urine explosion rather than the potential awkwardness of saying I might need to do a very natural thing. After a while, I hatched a master plan. I told him I needed to make an urgent call to my dad about my mortgage. 'Nobody questions mortgages,' I thought.

I took my handbag and went off into a bush. The relief was immense, it was one of those wees where you think you might never stop, where you're a bit surprised that you actually had that much fluid in you in the first place. Realising I didn't have any loo roll, I fished an old receipt out my bag, used it, folded it up and put it in the back pocket. Gross, but what was I meant to do? Relieved and smug with my wee-wee win, I went back to join him. 'Did you just take a slash in the bushes?' he asked. I hate the word 'slash'. I was indignant and denied it. 'You did,' he said, 'I just watched you do it! Minging!' I stood up, did the British thing of thanking him for a lovely time and called a taxi home. Weirdly, we didn't make it to the third date.

# Chapter 5

# Finding A Good Egg

At this point I think I have proved my qualifications in putting together the below list. Just a few things to watch out for. I am hoping it will be of help to you if ever you need it, or if you are happily settled, feel free to pass it on. I'm quite proud of it.

### The Louise Pentland Perils of Dating (Extremely Honest Edition)

- *If they don't respond immediately to my text or voicemail – They hate me. Or they are dead. Or as Billy Crystal says in When Harry Met Sally, they are trapped under something heavy. There are no other reasonable explanations for radio silence. I am thinking about them all the time, why aren't they thinking about me?*
- *If they respond immediately – They love me! They want to marry me. Time to start practising my name*

with their surname and Pinterest searching 'plus-size wedding dress'.

- It is normal to read into innocuous comments and assume they mean the worst. For example, if you receive a text from your date saying, 'Have a nice day', are they really saying, 'Have a nice life, you will never hear from me again'? Or are they wishing you a nice day up until the evening when you will meet and they will dump you, face to face? OR are they saying it because they really mean it because they are wildly in love with you and can't find the right words to say it so have just said that instead. No grey areas here in my mind.

- Adding a date as a friend on social media is BIG. I would happily sleep with someone before I would even consider letting them see my private Facebook page. That is a window to my soul and I am not prepared to be that exposed in front of them. See my bare bum hole, yes. Read all my Facebook statuses, no. (Again, sorry Dad.)

- Let them think you love sleeping in those thrush-inducing lace knickers, at least just for now. But bring back up jimjams. Treat yourself. We all know

*you want to sleep in your slightly stained My Little Pony pyjamas you bought five years ago in Primark but they don't need to know that.*

- *Poo perils. Go anywhere you can, but not the en suite. They have ears and they have noses and you don't want your business anywhere near either of those things. Go before you arrive at their house, go in a public loo at Euston station if you must (been there), but do not go in that teeny tiny poorly ventilated en suite bathroom.*

- *If you manage to make it through the first few dates then you are now at the next level of dating. This is the bit before you are officially a couple and cannot use the easy boyfriend/girlfriend tag. What do you call them in this interim stage? Answers on a postcard to me would be helpful because I haven't solved this one yet.*

The Beautiful American had faded away. Our non-relationship had been going on for two years and I couldn't stand the suspense any longer. I didn't have the time or energy to wait around and was focused on my number one priority, my gorgeous Darcy Doodles. It was time to move on from unrequited love and find myself a 'proper boyfriend'. You know, one that actually told you he was your boyfriend. In an ideal (and shallow) world, I'd have liked to have found one just in time for Valentine's Day, and guess what? It happened! Go me! Thing is though, things didn't quite go as I'd expected them to.

The night of 13th February several years ago, I went to dinner with some of the school mums. It was my first social event with them and I was thrilled that I had been included after waiting months to find a chink in their friendship armour. I had a great evening, we all hit it off, although I was a little intimidated by one of the mums. I couldn't remember her name (just so you all know, I do know it now and she's a really lovely lady!) but I did know her husband was called Julian and she was quite posh. So I called her 'Julian's Wife' in a quite posh, high-pitched voice – although only in my head, I didn't want her to think I was really weird. I wanted her to like me, I wanted to fit in with the Mums.

That night was my new boyfriend's birthday. He was having a pirate-themed party and sent me photos of him as a pirate which I shared joyfully with the table – mainly just because I was thrilled to actually have an official boyfriend! After dinner I jumped in a cab and joined him, stayed over and woke up there on Valentine's Day. Forgive the graphicness of this next bit but it is crucial to the story. Dad, probably best you just stop reading this book now. Pass it over to Tina (my stepmum) and let's never speak of this chapter again, OK?

So, we had sex and, as we finished, he looked down and said, 'Oh no . . . I don't know where the condom is!' Now, this is something NO WOMAN wants to hear. Utter panic! I frantically searched the duvet cover but, after a while, we realised where it was. It was . . . inside me and, to make matters worse, I had to try to fish it out in front of him. Yummy.

Despite my best efforts, I couldn't get it out. Being a gent, he offered to 'find it' for me. It was beyond mortifying. Although it was not quite as mortifying as standing in the middle of a huge supermarket with the only pharmacy open on a Sunday morning, still in last night's clothes that I wore to the Mummy Meetup Curry – sheer black top, tight jeans and high-heeled gold shoes – with slept-in make-up rubbed into my face and hair like a post-romp bush. No, hang on, let's make it worse. Let's bump into posh-voiced Julian's Wife at the till, paying for her wholesome Sunday roast ingredients while I am clutching a massive box that may as well say MORNING AFTER PILL on it! 'Oh hello,' she said, 'is this the pirate?' I wanted to slither under the conveyor belt and rip my own face off.

I think it's safe to say the next date didn't go well either. We had been dating for a while and having fun. The night before I was due to head off for a work trip we went out. I wanted to sit by a canal and have a few drinks but he was the boss of the relationship and decided we were going to take a walk in the forest. I was secretly in a foul mood (the type where if asked 'how are you?' you'll say 'fine' but really you mean 'fucking livid') – this was not my idea of a romantic evening and I had the wrong shoes on.

As we headed deeper into the woods, I started to feel uncomfortable. I wanted to turn back and he refused, he wanted to go deep, deep into the woods. On the path, I spotted a pair of glasses and, a bit further on, an abandoned shoe. In my defence, I'd been watching some spooky programmes on Netflix and I jumped to the only possible conclusion my brain had at the time. That someone had been murdered in these woods and my boyfriend was about to finish me off too. It was very logical at the time. I'd worked out his dastardly plan: here in the forest where nobody could hear me scream, he was going to kill me.

In his defence, he had never shown any signs of wanting to murder me and had actually always been quite nice to me. As he was striding ahead, I asked again if we could go back and he said he wanted to take a photo. Suddenly he stopped, turned around to look at me and I thought, 'Oh my God, this is it! I am going to be killed in these woods and I will never see my daughter again!' I turned and ran as fast as my fat little legs could carry me.

Back along the track, with brambles in my hair, I emerged back out onto the path a sweaty mess, straight into a group of ramblers. Their faces were filled with concern and they asked if I was OK. I suddenly felt a bit silly. I had no way of getting home so I just sat by my boyfriend's car and waited for him to come back. 'What are you doing?' he asked when he came out of the forest 20 minutes later. 'I thought you were going to murder me,' I mumbled. He looked horrified and took me home. He broke up with me soon after. Can't really blame him, I guess.

Throughout my chequered dating career I didn't introduce anyone to Darcy. I didn't want her to meet a new boyfriend only for him to disappear and be replaced a couple of months later (optimistic) by another. I had experienced this growing up when my dad had girlfriends and I knew I wanted to do things differently for Darcy.

There was one man. We had been dating for a while and it was coming up to my birthday. I was confident our relationship was going places so I tentatively considered him meeting Darcy. Before making any decisions or putting either of them in a position they weren't comfortable with, I sounded him out. He wasn't comfortable. No, he didn't want to meet her. He couldn't really handle me being a mum.

A few nights after I'd suggested he meet Darcy, he broke up with me. He said it was because I wasn't exciting or adventurous enough, which was ironic because I had just been to New York in my role as UN Ambassador for Gender Equality and the week before that, the Pope had invited me to the Vatican to talk about my YouTube channel (these things honestly happened), but hey, who am I to say what 'exciting' or 'adventurous' means? I think what he really meant was he didn't want me to be a mum.

He said if we had a child together it wouldn't be as special because I already had one. Even though we were quite clearly ill-matched and he wasn't good enough to be near my daughter if he felt this way, I suddenly felt devastated. I went to bed telling myself tomorrow would be a terrible day but, surprisingly, it wasn't. 'Maybe the next day will be awful and I'll miss him dreadfully,' I thought, but it wasn't bad at all and I didn't miss him. The terrible day never came.

Looking back, I know my heart wasn't in it, but sometimes when you've been alone and craved companionship for so long you tell yourself it's love and make the best of it. At the time, I thought he was a coward for not wanting to date a single mum but now I have a certain amount of respect for him. It was good that he told me before he met Darcy. She was totally unaffected and I'm really grateful to him for that.

It was the summer of 2016 when I 'retired' from the dating game. I didn't have the energy for it. It was hard work and relentlessly unsuccessful. Darcy and I were happy as a dynamic twosome. I obviously wasn't cut out to have an adult relationship and I pictured myself as an eccentric, interesting older woman. Turning into a Maggie Smith-style 'Lady in the Van' with my wonderful memories and many cats to keep me company in my twilight years. I deleted four of the five dating apps I had signed up to, which was also a relief because keeping up with them involved serious phone admin (that I'd refer to as 'checking my correspondence' so it sounded less like 'scrolling through the man market') that I didn't have time for. I was happy as we were; we didn't need anyone else in our gang to complete us.

One day, though, while waiting in the school car park to collect Darcy and with not much else to do, I decided to have just the tiniest scroll on Tinder. Oops.

There was a lovely man but he had no bio, which went against all my rules of online dating. I was proud of my Tinder bio – it was comedy gold, it was witty, it said a lot. I was actually so into the bio side of things I'd offer to write them for my friends, so I was suspicious of those who didn't have one. But something about this guy made me swipe. He swiped back. Then we messaged. I think I said something like, 'Why no bio, Mr Mystery?' and he quipped back something about waiting for me to ask for it. It was funny at the time (or maybe I was just a bit more lonely than I thought, ha) and it was enough to start a conversation rolling. He asked me out for a drink. I figured I wasn't going to change my single status and grand plan, but a girl has to have the odd glass of wine, right? It was something to do on a Thursday night at least.

That evening, I was medium-level nervous and by this point I was quite the expert on first dates. I knew the drill and I knew which outfit would work. I plumped for a white dress and mint cardigan combo with killer red lipstick – that's how much I thought it'd be just a quick drink. If I'd have thought there'd be some smooching in the car park, I'd never have gone for a full red lip!

As I was about to leave the house, Aunty Judith turned up because she was having a Bad Day and needed to tell me all about it. Judith is obviously more important than any man I might be flirting with on Tinder so I was listening to her, but in my head I was starting to worry about being a tiny bit late. My date sent me a text: 'I'm here!' I felt terrible having to cut Judith short and be late for my Man of Mystery but she offered to drive me and we chatted en route. Now she holds this like a badge of honour. 'Yes, I was there from the start! I drove her to the date!' she tells people. God, I love her.

I turned up at the pub – one of those trendy ones with filament bulbs and wood everywhere. There was Liam, secretly relieved that I was late because he'd perhaps been a bit more nervous than he thought and needed a moment to down a giant glass of water (it was a boiling summer day) and cool his jets a bit. We clicked instantly. The conversation flowed, there were no awkward silences and I felt so comfortable in his company.

Liam was older than me, had a great job and seemed a jolly good egg. He was kind, patient, funny, intelligent, attractive and had lovely manners (a good foundation to a great man). In the past, I had been through the roller coaster of emotions with Brad, the tedium of hopeless first dates and the disappointment of ill-matched relationships. Suddenly here was someone stable and strong who was interested in me for who I really was. It felt grown-up. He seemed like a man, not a boy.

Funny pre-date story for you. I had a bit of a system with men, which was before I'd go for a date I'd FaceTime them. You can tell a lot about a person from their tone of voice and body language and I think you can glean a bit of this from video calls, so it was a good vetting practice. Plus, I'm pretty confident in front of a camera thanks to ten years of vlogging, so it was a nice way for me to ease into a new person.

We talked for over an hour and Liam, naturally, asked what I did. I said I was an author and talked a bit about the books I've written. What I didn't share, though, was the vlogging, blogging and everything in between. Firstly, it's a bit of a strange job and secondly, I knew if he looked me up, he'd know SO much about me and I knew so little about him, it felt majorly imbalanced. So, I said, 'I know this sounds really suspicious but PLEASE don't Google me before our date. It's nothing bad but I just want the opportunity for us both to be on equal footing and if you Google me, we won't be.' Liam, being the gent that he is, looked absolutely bewildered but promised not to. I told him exactly what I do on our date, and by this time we had totally clicked, so I asked him what he'd thought about my bizarre request. Turns out, he put 'confident' and 'secretive online' together and came up with DOMINATRIX. We still laugh about that!

It turned out Liam had been living five minutes from my house for years and yet we had never crossed paths and had no mutual friends. Nothing seemed to faze him. On our third date, he came with me to the premiere of *Bridget Jones's Baby* and calmly walked the red carpet, coping with the bank of photographers and being thrust into a very different type of experience. I loved his combined sense of adventure and security. Isn't that what we are all looking for in our perfect partner? Plus, he was HOT. This was all going awfully well.

I was still reeling from being dumped by my previous boyfriend because of Darcy, so I was exceptionally clear with Liam. The first thing I told him was that I was a mum and that Darcy would always come first. Liam didn't have children of his own but he completely understood. A few weeks later, after a string of brilliant dates together, he was driving past my house and asked if he could pop in. I was in the garden with Aunty Judith and Darcy, totally unprepared, but my intuition said yes.

It helped that Judith was there too. I introduced him to Darcy as 'my friend Liam', we all had a bit of time in the garden and he left. It was relaxed, happy and natural. We planned a day trip to a butterfly farm a few weeks after and I asked Darcy if we should invite my friend Liam too and she said yes. We were careful not to be affectionate in front of her or give her any reason to feel insecure and we just had a lot of fun. Everything felt so natural and easy.

For a while, I spent my non-Darcy days with Liam and focused on Darcy when she was with me. I knew Liam and I were falling for each other so it was time to take the next step. I have never felt like I am only a mother half of the week when I am with Darcy and I don't live two halves of a life. Liam knew this. But Darcy had only met him a couple of times as 'Mummy's friend'. How would she feel if I told her that he was my boyfriend and was going to be around for some of the time we were both together? I asked her if she liked him, knowing already that she did, and then I said that he had become my boyfriend and how did she feel about that? She was happy. It felt like a weight lifted from my shoulders and Liam and I could move our relationship forward.

One of the things I am most proud of is the strong bond between Liam and Darcy – how much time and care he gave her and, in return, how she received this and accepted him into our lives. If this hadn't been the case, Liam and I would not be together now. I talk about how to approach this step-parent relationship later in the book – I don't claim to know everything but I know what we did worked for us. They have the loveliest relationship – they play jokes on each other, watch rugby together and enjoy hanging out. Liam was the one who taught Darcy to swim and he comes to her school parents' evenings with me. He has invested in her life and our life together as a family and (another spoiler) when Pearl arrived this further cemented it. If he puts money into Pearl's savings account he does the same for Darcy. I asked him recently what he says to people who ask how many children he has. Two, he said, he is a father of two. Darcy is a lucky little girl.

One of my favourite memories of the three of us is the day we set fire to a restaurant. Not on purpose, of course – we weren't a family of pyromaniacs. It was Mother's Day. Of course it was; it couldn't just be a standard, run-of-the-mill, popping-out-for-a-bite-to-eat, low-key sort of day. Liam took Darcy and I out for a lovely lunch at a bistro pub, full of families celebrating their brilliant mums. We were settled into a cosy corner and had just worked our way through a platter of scallops – Darcy loves them, pretty unusual for a then-five-year-old, I know. I felt loved, happy and relaxed. I was focused on a conversation with Liam when Darcy suddenly piped up, 'Look, Mummy, fire!' There was a small candle on our table and Darcy had inadvertently put her napkin on it. I am assuming it was an accident because she has never done it before or since. She has always loved eating out and behaved well in those situations so I am giving her the benefit of the doubt. Alternatively, being a small child, she could have decided to see what sort of fire her napkin would create. I will never know and I didn't stop to interrogate her at the time because there were flames rapidly spreading in front of me. There was a fire!

My first instinct was to push Darcy back from it and then attempt to blow the fire out, with big puffs like I was blowing out candles on a birthday cake. The fire was TOO BIG for this though and, as I blew, I sent embers across the table and onto a stack of paper menus that immediately started to burn. This was no time to be understated. I saw everyone around me calmly tucking into their roast lamb, oblivious to the unfolding drama, and in my head I shouted 'FIRE! FIRE! FIRE!' In fact, it wasn't in my head, I shouted it out loud while grabbing Darcy and trying to move back from the inferno. It was like being in a film where everyone suddenly moves at the same time in panic and fear!

This entire debacle had taken less than a minute. Liam, my hero, was unsuccessfully trying to quell the flames before sweeping the fire onto the floor with his bare arm and attempting to stamp it out with his feet. The people to one side of us were hemmed in by the incident, clutching their children and watching on in horror. At that point, Liam's laces started to catch fire and another table close to us raised their wine glasses, offering to tip them onto the flames. 'Shall we?!' they asked, but I wasn't sure dousing the fire with a good Chardonnay was a sensible decision.

Just as Liam had the fire under control, managing to save his shoes, the waiting staff pitched up. They eyed us suspiciously and, instead of asking if we were OK, they said, 'Oh! What's happened?' 'A fire,' I said, quite fraught. 'There has been a FIRE is what has happened, a whole flipping fire.' 'Oh,' they said, 'is it out?' I said yes and we all looked at each other, unsure what the etiquette was in these sorts of situations. 'Would you like the dessert menu?' they asked. 'Um, yes, OK then.' We all sat back down and ordered sticky toffee pudding while the ashes just lay on the floor by Liam's burnt laces. Happy Mother's Day!

# Chapter 6

# The Story of Pearl: Best Bonus Baby

Let's recap slightly and go back to the first date I had with Liam. Specifically, the conversation about children. Which is a pretty unusual topic on first meeting, but when you are dating at this age there's no point playing games – I was 31, already a mum, and he was 39. I told him about Darcy, he was completely cool and said it was exactly what he would expect from 30-something's dating – how refreshing. He also said he would really love to be a father. I hadn't really thought about it from that perspective, after shutting down the idea of a second child when I was midway through giving birth to the first. I realised with a jolt of surprise that I wasn't opposed to the idea.

The first six months of our relationship sped past. We were happy, in love and I began to feel those familiar twinges of broodiness that grew stronger as time wore on. I started to picture life with a baby, a new pram caught my eye, I thought what a wonderful big sister Darcy would be and when Aunty Judith popped over to see my new house, she said, 'Oh, just imagine a toddler on this lawn.'

I started to imagine it and couldn't stop. Worried about frightening Liam off but needing to voice it, I said, 'I know this sounds crazy as we've only been together seven months but I am broody . . . does it scare you?!' 'I've been broody for years,' he said calmly. We decided to park the idea for the rest of the year and talk again further down the line. A month later I was pregnant. Oh.

I was on a big photoshoot for industry magazine favourite *Blogosphere* and it was my first front cover. I had been thrilled to be asked and arrived at the shoot location full of excitement. I also felt a bit odd – maybe the adrenalin was to blame but I felt a bit chilly, I was shivering. 'I'm probably pregnant,' I joked to one of my team and then I stopped still. Oh. My. God. When was my last period? I needed to find a pregnancy test kit. But first I had to pose in a raunchy, sheer top with wet-look hair, pressed up against the glass of a stately home orangery for goodness' sake. Throughout the shoot, as the photographer was asking for 'sultry eyes' and 'sexy thoughts', I was thinking about baby travel systems and whether I would need to change my car.

I went home via the chemist. Liam was on a late shift so I didn't want to text him. 'It will probably be a false alarm, no point making a big deal of it, I'll just do the test and put my mind at rest,' I reasoned. There were two faint lines. I was pregnant. My first thought was joy and my second thought was realising that I had done this test alone without Liam. I had denied him the experience of waiting for the result. OK, not to worry, I would just have to lie and pretend I was doing it for the first time with him – nothing like a massive moment in your life to test your acting skills.

When he came home, I turned in an Oscar-winning performance, starting with, 'Babe, my period's a bit late,' to, 'Sure it's nothing, but let's do a quick test,' to, 'No, you look, I can't.' Liam turned the pregnancy test over and studied the little window. His face fell. 'No, you're not pregnant,' he said sadly. 'Really?' I squeaked, 'are you sure?!' 'Yes babe,' he said, shaking his head slowly, shoulders slumped. 'REALLY?!!' I said. 'Take. Another. Look.' He held the test out to me. 'You're reading it wrong! Two lines means I AM pregnant,' and I pulled the previous test out to prove it. We were both ecstatic. 'Is it too soon?' I asked him. 'No,' he said, 'when you know, you know.'

I call Pearl my Bonus Baby. I didn't think I would have more than one child so I was over the moon. I booked my first midwife appointment and there was Julia, the same midwife who had been with me for Darcy. The memories came flooding back. The horror, fear and shame from my previous birth hit me like a ton of bricks. This certainly wasn't Julia's fault but seeing her again was enough to trigger my anxiety – I had to get this baby out at some point, but how? I sure as hell wasn't going to go through what I had first time around. Things went downhill mentally after that. I spent a lot of time crying, too scared to think clearly. This wasn't helped by a constant feeling of nausea and being so unbelievably tired – not just a bit snoozy but properly bone-tired. A supermarket shop was enough to wear me out for the rest of the day.

At this point, what I didn't need was a trip to Disneyland Paris, but it was already booked and I couldn't bear to let Darcy down. I was only a couple of months pregnant so hadn't told anyone and was trying to Continue As Normal. Keep Calm and Carry On, as they say.

I had a horrible experience while we were there that's stayed with me all these years as an example of how rubbish people and the internet can be. I should caveat now that usually I think people and the internet are amazing, obviously, but this taught me a harsh lesson.

I was in the middle of Disneyland, ironically in Fantasyland, where I felt very far from living any kind of fantasy, I was really sickly (nothing says 'first trimester' like vomming up a Nutella crêpe near the Peter Pan ride) and had to head back to the hotel, where I sat forlornly on the lobby sofa, unable to move any further without wanting to throw up again. A woman strode up and told me her daughter wanted a photo with me because she'd recognised me from YouTube. There was no 'hello' or nice chit-chat, just, that's what she wanted. It took all the energy I didn't have to say how sorry I was, but I really wasn't very well and would she mind if I didn't? This was not at all what she wanted to hear. She launched into a huffy attack, telling me how incredibly rude I was for not doing what she wanted. By this point, I was almost in tears because I hate confrontation. I was sweaty, trying not to physically move my tummy in any way and my hormones were all over the place. I said I was sorry and told her really quietly that I was secretly pregnant. She walked off. I assumed with understanding.

When I arrived home so many people knew about my pregnancy. The woman had gone online and posted a comment about how rude I was and then announced I was eight weeks pregnant. It was a nasty, unkind retaliation for not getting what she wanted. She took away my moment of telling friends and family my happy news. Although it was a really low thing of her to do (hi if you're reading this book!), I'm thankful. It taught me to guard my private life and guard my daughters because you can't hold everyone to your own standards and not everyone is a good egg.

As the days wore on my anxiety continued and I knew I had to give myself a good talking-to. I reasoned that there were ways to mitigate what had happened last time. I was just going to pay for a private hospital, book in for a C-section and erase all those awful memories in one straightforward labour. As the mean woman from Paris had outed me already, I made a video announcing my pregnancy at 11 weeks. It felt safe enough by then to talk about it openly, I was beginning to feel a bit better and was cheered by my Caesarean plan. The excitement came flooding back once I had shared the news officially and then it became actual news across media networks. The next day I started bleeding. The idea I could be losing my baby was awful enough without the added pressure that it might be on BBC News.

I rang Liam and asked him to come straight home. I rang Julia and asked her to come over too. I just want to jump in here and sing Julia's praises. She didn't have to come over, that wasn't required of her, but she did out of her own time. I'll always be grateful for that compassion. Julia, if you ever read this, you're amazing. OK, back to the awful bleeding. I wasn't sure what else to do in the face of a possible miscarriage but lying down seemed to be sensible. I reasoned that if I lay on my back with my legs up then gravity would keep the baby in.

Julia made an appointment for me to have an emergency ultrasound at the hospital that afternoon. We sat anxiously in the waiting room, watching the clock as the minutes ticked by. It wasn't the usual waiting room full of happy couples looking forward to seeing their babies for the first or second time. This was the waiting room for problem scans, for those of us who were emergencies, wishing on everything we had that the news would be good.

Lying on the hospital bed while the ultrasound tried to find the baby was the lowest moment and the longest minute of my life. I braced myself for the doctor to tell me there was no heartbeat. I kept looking at Liam – he might lose the baby he had wanted forever and it would be my fault because I was the one responsible for looking after it. Was it because I had done too much, worked too hard, walked around Disneyland Paris? Maybe it was punishment for not giving the ghastly woman a photograph.

Then, to my absolutely joy, the doctor found the heartbeat. She checked me over and said it was blood from somewhere else. Everything was fine, the baby was alive. To this day, I'm not sure where the blood was coming from, but I didn't care: I wasn't miscarrying, the baby was safe. As I left, she told me not to return unless blood was 'gushing', which thankfully it never did. I walked out full of gratitude that all was well and full of sadness for those who might not have been as lucky as me that day.

This was a turning point – the first in a couple of big gear changes that allayed my fears and refocused my energy. I was so grateful that all was well and that I could put a plan in place to deal with childbirth that I promised myself I would stop worrying. The test results came back from the Harmony clinic, where I had gone for an early scan. They reiterated that the baby was healthy and that I was having a girl! We had asked to find out and the news came at just the right time. I was thrilled. I was already a girl mummy so I knew I was well prepared for another. Liam would have been happy with either but had confessed he was hoping for a girl. Darcy was going to have a sister!

When I was 12 weeks pregnant we sat Darcy down. She knew I hadn't been feeling very well and I didn't want her to worry unnecessarily. She was only six so we kept it simple: there was a baby in Mummy's tummy, she was going to be a big sister and we were all thrilled about it. She was over the moon. A while later, thoughtful and quiet, she came up to me and asked me how the baby had made it into my tummy. Slightly thrown by her question, I used the classic parent technique and threw it back to her. 'How do you think it happened?' I asked. She told me she had wished for it. 'Then your wish has come true,' I said, although I knew this was going to cause me problems when she wished for other things and expected those to be granted too!

I talked to Julia about struggling mentally with the thought of labour and how I was trying to keep the flashbacks from Darcy's birth under control. I announced firmly that I was going to have a planned C-section in a private hospital as I thought this would alleviate my concerns. I joked that I would also be given a glass of champagne and a cream tea as part of the package. Actually, that wasn't much of a joke, that was one of the things I was most excited about at the hospital I'd seen on a TV documentary about celeb births.

Julia – this wonderful woman who had delivered more babies than I could ever imagine – listened sympathetically and said she understood. She also said that booking in a Caesarean was not the easy option; it was a big operation and I needed to seriously consider this. She also mentioned PTSD, the first time I had heard of it, and suggested I might be affected by it. I Googled it and immediately recognised the description and symptoms – it was a weird relief. Julia also introduced me to a friend of hers, Jane, a private midwife who could be on hand to look after me throughout my pregnancy and labour, which was something I really wanted because I knew, with the way the NHS is organised, that I wouldn't have Julia at my delivery. I desperately wanted familiarity and consistency so this seemed like a good option.

Jane came to my house and, like Julia, she listened to me. She went through all the options and asked me if I had ever thought about a home birth. I did well not to spit my drink out all over my growing bump! 'Are you out of your damned mind?' I thought. 'I can't possibly sign up for that, not after last time and all the medication and intervention I needed.'

Jane knew I was sceptical. She made an appointment for a Meet the Matron session, so we could go through my notes from the first birth and understand what had gone wrong. I mentioned this earlier and I really can't recommend it highly enough. I sat in front of her, 24 weeks pregnant, and I cried. I couldn't stop. She talked through Darcy's birth, admitted mistakes had been made, she apologised on behalf of the NHS and she told me that a change in policy meant these things would not be repeated. Hearing that from a professional was incredible. I hadn't been oversensitive, I wasn't making a fuss, I shouldn't have been expected to get on with it because 'that's just what birth is'. My terrible experience was validated as such and, little did I know it at the time, this was the first step in my recovery.

I appreciated every single thing she said to me but the damage was done. How could she be sure it wouldn't happen again? I couldn't breathe properly in the hospital and when I walked past the ward I had been in six years before, my heart raced. I made another appointment with the Matron Paula to talk more about PTSD and then Jane took me up to the new birthing suite. It was midwife-led, much less clinical than the last place, and she wanted to show me as it was an option. I had a panic attack. I can count on one hand the number of attacks I have had in my life and this was one of them. I walked into the room with the handwashing signs, the blue plastic hospital flooring and the yellow bins for needles and I totally lost it. My legs were shaking and I felt like I didn't know where to look, I so badly didn't want to be in that room. Jane was fantastic. I was an absolute mess, sobbing, apologising, vulnerable, I just had to get out. As we left, she said calmly that everything available in the birthing suite could be at home with me if I wanted a home birth.

Liam and I talked about the options. He supported any decision I made; it was my body and my choice and he would be there regardless. He had been there at the lowest points of my pregnancy and he hadn't shied away from any of my tears, anxiety or concerns.

As I talked to my midwives, I could feel myself beginning to make peace. I needed to allow myself to heal. Around the same time, a vlogger friend of mine, Hannah Michalak, had just had her baby using the hypnobirthing technique. I contacted her and her husband and asked them what they thought. They couldn't speak highly enough of the experience, or of Siobhan Miller from the Positive Birth Company, who had led them through it. They said she was a goddess in their house. I need to meet this goddess I thought, maybe she will hold the key to me finally having a birth experience that didn't scare the absolute living daylights out of me.

I have to admit, before she arrived, I had visions of a beautiful hippy in patchwork skirts, wafting incense around me, perhaps even whipping out a small harp to play a calming melody while I sat cross-legged and feeling my inner calm or something. I know, this is an incredibly stereotypical thought, but I need to show you how removed I was from this sort of lifestyle. I thought, 'It really won't be very "me" but I have no choice. I have one giant baby and one small (let me think it is at least) opening and somehow one's gotta get through the other.' If a harp and some meditation were going to sort this out, I was on board, incense and all!

When Siobhan left, after an educational, interesting and supportive chat involving science, pre-natal facts and positive language, I felt such utter peace. I learnt more from her in one meeting than I had in my two pregnancies and one labour. Think of me what you will, but I did not know that the uterus was a muscle, hence the word 'contraction' as it endeavours to work the baby out. Except we weren't to use that word and instead describe it as a 'surge'. No painful contractions, thank you, just powerful surges. Jane and Paula were completely on board with hypnobirthing, which was important for me because I wanted them there. I was going to have a home birth and we didn't even need a harp (though my friend Esther did offer to come and play one quietly in the corner of the room. Rest assured, I politely declined)!

While I was finding solutions for my PTSD and birth fears, I was secretly battling a severe case of sadness. Logically, I knew how lucky I was and how much I wanted this second child but my head couldn't make my heart feel better. I went through much of the pregnancy feeling flat, grey and bland. I cried a lot. I convinced myself it was down to hormones and perfectly normal to feel this way. It was only when a couple of my friends, Emma and Jess, sat me down and said they were worried about me that I stopped to think.

It wasn't normal to be upset over unloading a dishwasher – anything and everything seemed to set me off. I felt like a complete failure not to be coping.

Every time somebody asked me how I was I said 'fine' in a cheery manner. How many times have women used that word to cover up the fact that they are the opposite of fine? How could I be so low when I had so much – a gorgeous daughter, another on the way, a wonderful partner, a great career and a happy home? It didn't make sense. I was embarrassed, ashamed even, to admit I was struggling.

Here's a little story that sums up that time. A window into how I was feeling. I was seven months pregnant and had taken Darcy to the park with Liam. It was one of those glorious sunny, crisp autumn days, with bright blue skies when it feels good to be alive. I didn't notice that though. I didn't even take an Instagram of the golden leaves against the aforementioned blue sky, that's how bad it was. I sat on the bench in the park while Darcy played and collected conkers to bring home with us. I had nothing to carry them back in so I let her fill up my woollen gloves with them. Suddenly I began to cry. I don't know where it came from and I didn't make a habit of doing it in public but I was fully there. I was sat on a bench, heavily pregnant and sobbing, holding psychotic-looking woollen hands that dangled between my legs like udders.

Liam put his arm around me and asked me what was wrong. 'I'm just sad all the time,' I choked. 'Every day I wake up sad, shower, dress, keep on top of things, but I am just so sad.' My crying had become snotty and I wiped my nose on the conker-stuffed lumpy gloves, leaving a snail trail of snot – yummy. Liam said simply, 'Maybe you are a bit depressed and that's OK because we can fix it.'

It doesn't sound much but that moment made a big difference to me. I look back now and wonder why I held it all in for so long. Telling Liam, speaking it out loud, felt like a total release. It was as though someone had seen me, completely. If he said we could fix it, we could fix it. One of Siobhan's little affirmation quotes she shared with me was, 'My birthing partner is by my side and on my side.' Liam was truly on my side. As for my poor stretched gloves, they have never been the same again.

Pearl was due on 28th December. For those days leading up to it and just beyond we waited, happily distracted by Christmas. As we entered January, the hospital consultants started to twitch. They were not happy about my home birth decision, they wanted to book me in for a C-section and kept reminding me of the trauma of my first birth. I was being scanned regularly because of high BMI and at each session the consultant would take the opportunity to advise a medical delivery. My hypnobirth practice had taught me to ask why, so I did. There was reference to me being overweight, the baby might be too big, what if I haemorrhaged again?

Each time I had the conversation I could feel my resolve weakening and I had to speak to Jane to reassure me. I lived a few minutes from the hospital so if something did go wrong I could be there in a flash. I understood how hard it was for the NHS to tailor their care to each individual but I couldn't put myself in that situation again if I had another option. I was grateful that they would be there if anything went wrong but couldn't I just try and hope that I wouldn't need them?

In the end, I stopped attending my hospital appointments. To be clear, I don't advise anyone else does that but it is what I did. The consultant had become unpleasant. I completely understand she had a job to do and she had to follow protocol, but I felt terrible after each visit. On one occasion, I was put in a room and had groin samples taken to check I wasn't carrying a disease in prep for a C-section I had refused to have. Nobody there was listening to me, they were intent on box-ticking exercises. They insisted on booking me in for the op even though I told them I would not be turning up for it. It seemed a ridiculous waste of resources. I reassured them each time that if my midwife felt there was any danger at all I would be straight in, but they didn't seem to take my wishes on board. I didn't want to put Pearl in danger but I also knew I had the right to at least try this.

On 11th January, I called the hospital to remind them I wouldn't be there for the C-section they had booked that day. 'It's your choice but if your placenta fails . . .' they said ominously. I tried not to think about worst-case scenarios, I just tried to be rational about every eventuality. That's quite tricky though when you're two weeks overdue and you haven't moved in anything other than a slow and difficult waddle for about a month. Anyone reading this who's in their last month of pregnancy – I salute you!

On the night of 13th January, I went to bed and was woken by little surges, light enough to be Braxton Hicks, so I went back to sleep. By 1am I was awake. Hello, I thought, we are in business and, weirdly, a wave of calm came over me. With Darcy, I had been in complete terror; this time around I was safe and at home with a hypnobirthing plan for both me and Liam. I was in control, I was ready.

I woke Liam up and we hung out in the kitchen for a while, talking about how soon we'd be holding our darling daughter and what a wild ride this last year had been. It was lovely to be so present with each other and talk about the big things like that. I did my breathing exercises, sitting on my birthing ball, chatting as he emptied the dishwasher. There was no drama or panic and we called Jane at 3am.

Now, this book is honest and so I do have to say, labour was painful. At one point I was sick in my mixing bowl (the one downside to a homebirth – you have to puke in your own stuff) while I was having a surge (which definitely is a better word, in my opinion, for contraction) and that wasn't super fun. I have not found the secret to a natural, pain-free birth but if I do, I'll be sure to let you know! I am not a 'natural earth mother', I did ask for a full body anaesthetic several times and I know I swore a lot. But it *was* also manageable and I could control it without the need for drugs. I could deal with each surge, breathe through it and then relax in between them. The power of the mind is a truly amazing thing. I used my own bathroom, could choose who was there with me and felt empowered by such a dignified experience. No splayed vagina to the world and his wife this time around, no fingers all up in bits I wasn't wanting them to be in, no beeping machines, no wires, no needles.

At about 6am, I asked Jane to examine me. Nobody forced me to be examined, it was my choice. I was 7cm dilated. This baby was not far off. By 8.30am, I was feeling sleepy and had what felt like a part nap, part Zen-like state of relaxation. I was vaguely aware of people in the room but I was also dreaming that I was in Courchevel, skiing down a mountain with my manager Maddie, swish, swish. The cold flannel I was holding in real life became a snowball in my dream.

I had floated off into an amazing hallucination and woke an hour later ready to have the baby. As I write this, I know it sounds unbelievable. If someone had told me this would be my birth experience I'd have laughed but, I promise you, skiing. Lovely! Perhaps I'll go there for real one day!

At 9.55am I climbed into the birthing pool. Pearl was born at 10.03am. I held her to me and waited for things to go wrong, panicked for the first time in my labour and delivery. This was the point the consultant had warned me about. I might haemorrhage like I did with Darcy. Maybe the pool would fill with blood and they'd have to ring the ambulance. They'd have to take Pearl out of my arms and heave me out the pool. Except, that didn't happen.

I carried on holding my beautiful newly-born baby and there was minimal blood loss. I delivered the placenta intact. The actual worst part was getting out of the birthing pool. I was like one big, slippery naked eel with a sore fanny, holding onto a tiny slippery naked eel, trying to climb out of a paddling pool onto a tiled floor. That was about as dangerous as things got. I walked, with dignity, to the sofa with my baby, swaddled in towels and my dressing gown, and she fed immediately. I had a slight tear from where I had torn with Darcy but we decided to let it heal naturally.

Voila. A beautiful, happy, home birth. If I could have physically done a bow, I would have.

## What Not to Say to New Mums

1. Enjoy this time because it goes so quickly – yes, we know this. We are very aware that it's a blink of an eye between cleaning up baby-milk sick and teenage cider-induced vomit. Telling a new mum this puts her under even more pressure not to say anything negative about her experience and to feel bad about not cherishing every (sometimes rather tiring) moment.

2. You are so lucky – similar to the above. Bringing a healthy baby home is the best feeling in the world and every new mum knows things could have been different. They hold gratitude in their hearts every single minute but it doesn't mean they don't also think they have made the biggest mistake of their lives at 4am in the morning when they have had no sleep.

3. Looking forward to getting back into your jeans? –meaning, when are you going to lose your baby weight? 'Fuck off' is the best answer to this or any other question that sounds vaguely like, 'When are you going to lose weight?'

4. That baby is the spitting image of its father – yes, it may be, yes, you may fear you have just cloned your partner, but you have also just been through hell and back to birth this being. It must have something that is vaguely similar to you. Knees? Nostrils? A dimple for God's sake? If you really can't see any of Mum's features, just ooh and ahh and say he or she is the cutest little pudding you've ever seen. Easy!

5. Is that how they do it these days? – in reference to sleeping, feeding, winding, whatever it may be. Unless you really do know exactly what you're talking about, don't add more fear, worry and late-night over-googling.

6. Aren't you breastfeeding? – I have covered this elsewhere but I do like to repeat myself just in case those at the back weren't listening. If you cannot breastfeed for whatever reason then do not feel the weight of the guilt from others' judgement. Remember that Fed is Best.

7. Surely you won't go back to work? – yes, no, maybe, if you want to or have to. Right now, you are still coming to terms with something the size

of a large melon coming out of your body so you really don't need to make any decisions.

8. When are you going back to work? – like the above, there is an assumption that you should do something. Judgey McJudgers, move on.

9. Tell me all the gory details about the birth! – you don't need to share everything, just the parts you are comfortable with recounting. Or suggest that you talk about it another time. Preferably when you aren't sitting on a rubber ring or attempting to shove your nipple in your baby's mouth.

10. I think your baby is tired/hungry/uncomfortable/has wind – ignore unsolicited parenting advice. You know your baby better than anybody, especially a busybody.

11. You can kiss goodbye to sleep! – you know this, we all know this, we do not need someone to gleefully tell us how hard it is. We are living it. We know.

12. When will you have another one? – I don't really need to respond to this, do I?!

13. *Is that a dummy? – it could mean they approve or they really don't. Either way, the choice is yours.*

14. *What do you do all day? Arghhhh.*

15. *Enjoy your time off! – Ahahahahaha. LOLs.*

*DO SAY – Oh, you brave, amazing, clever, clever woman! Here's a casserole for this evening, now give me the baby and you go have a little nap or bath or Insta-scroll! Love you!*

Liam was amazing. I could not have done it without him. Throughout the labour he had done exactly what I had asked of him. He had respected my choices, looked after me and the midwives and filled the pool. Once Pearl had arrived and I was in a nest on the sofa, he poured drinks and made bagels for us all before the midwives left. Saying goodbye and thank you to Jane and Paula was emotional – they had given me the strength to believe I could do it.

When it was just the three of us, we looked at each other. What do we do now?! We didn't have any paracetamol which I knew I would be needing so Liam said he would pop out and pick up a McDonald's on the way back. But hang on! I had just had a baby, should I be left alone? What if I needed the loo (bit stingy right after birth) or if Pearl was really crying and I couldn't cope? I don't know why I suddenly felt so insecure but I'd only been out the pool a couple of hours and I wasn't ready to be left. I did really need some paracetamol though (vaginal tear – ouch) so we decided to ring my friend Clare, who happened to be enjoying a Sunday roast in the local pub. 'Hi, I've just had a baby,' I literally said, 'at home, actually. Would you mind coming over so Liam can pop out?' She was incredulous and with me ten minutes later. I wonder how many calls she'll have like that in her life!

I stayed on the sofa, wrapped up in blankets and my dressing gown, till bedtime. Holding a soft, snuggly Pearl close, skin-to-skin contact all day, only moving to go to the loo (invest in a squeezy bidet bottle, pregnant ladies – Google it, you'll thank me, I promise). Darcy came home in the evening and met Pearl for the first time. She didn't spot her initially under the blankets and when she did, she just said simply, 'Oh, my sister!' with such glee it was incredible. It was a moment to cherish. I caught it on camera and it's one of my favourite bits of footage I've ever recorded. Liam and I sat there till 1am chatting, talking about the day's events and marvelling at our beautiful new baby. We had spent 15 uninterrupted, private, peaceful hours together and what a way for Pearl to spend her first day in the world. I finally started to understand the 'baby bliss' people talk about.

The following morning I showered, dressed and put my make-up on. I know a lot of people will be horrified reading that because we're all advised to stay in bed and PJs. I understand. I'd actually say the same to a friend that had just given birth but it's just not me. Putting my make-up on feels good. It makes me feel at my best and that's what I wanted. It wasn't strenuous, it only took five minutes and I felt accomplished – you can't argue with that. Well, you probably could but please don't, ha!

As we'd had a homebirth we had to take Pearl to the GP to be checked over by a doctor and after that we popped to the supermarket for some treats – felt like I deserved some!

It was another really beautiful, blissful day but when we arrived home we remembered there was still a jacuzzi-size pool of bloody water in the middle of the dining room to deal with. Liam said it was no problem, he could easily deal with it and decided to siphon it out with a hose. This could have been a disaster but he managed to do this part without a horrific accidental swallowing incident. After he'd removed most of the water with the hose, he was left with 10 per cent of the gory dregs swishing about in the bottom of the birthing pool so he decided to drag it into the garden and pour it onto the flower beds – how nutritious for them!

I watched from the patio doors, cuddling Pearl, as he manhandled the pool out across the lawn in the pouring rain. Suddenly he staggered and slipped on the wet grass, tipping the contents of the pool all over him. I've never seen a man go so pale so quickly. 'Are you OK, babe?' I asked, trying to hide my laughter. 'Yep, all OK,' he said through gritted teeth, placenta smears over his new white trainers. We still laugh about that now, though maybe I do harder and longer than he does.

There was another underlying issue that had tweaked my depression in both Darcy's early months and Pearl's pregnancy. I was supressing long-held anxieties linking to my childhood and a period of immense unhappiness I suffered at the hands of a close family friend. Yep, things are about to get heavy. I knew this was rumbling on in the far and dusty recesses of my mind but I was yet to face it full-on. Let's do that now. Are you with me?

# Chapter 7

# Tough Times

Immediate trigger warning. If you are looking for my usual LOLs and bants in this chapter there won't be much of that, so apologies now. It has taken all my nerve to write this down as it is the first time I have shared this part of my childhood fully. It's a hard read but it's a really important one, so I hope you stick with it. It's the story of how I came to be who I am and the lessons I learnt that have made me a better mother. I promise there is a happy ending and I'll try to pop a few punchlines in too because, you know me, never knowingly under-funny. Deep breaths, here goes.

After Mum died, and I don't mean months after but a few days later, my dad invited a woman over for coffee on Christmas Day. They were just friends but, even to my untrained seven-year-old eye, I sensed it could be more than that. The woman, let's call her Sandra, was very nice to me. She was too nice to me, over-friendly in a false way. How adults are when they don't like children but pretend they do, so that the adults who do like children don't suspect a thing. There are books and movies full of this type of chilling character and nothing good ever comes of them but, for a while, before they are stopped, they manage to seriously damage the children in the story.

Some time after, Sandra and my dad started seeing each other and she would shower me with gifts of sweets, clothes and make-up. It was ostentatious behaviour and it made me feel uncomfortable. She was so different from my mum – younger, uber glamorous and there was nothing mumsy or maternal about her. It wasn't long before she had moved in and was around every day. My dad worked away from home a lot, often travelling for two weeks at a time, so it was just her and me rattling around a big house with nothing in common, waiting for my dad to come home. I was in her care all the time.

At first, Sandra would make little unkind comments about me and my aunts. I was confused – I adored them so didn't understand what she could take issue with. She started to make it hard for me to see them; I felt isolated and desperately missed my mum. The subtle jibes grew.

She told me cancer was caused by stress and mothers got stressed by naughty children. I was only seven but I knew what she was saying. She was telling me my mother's death was my fault, that the stress caused by my supposed naughtiness had given her cancer. I was confused because my dad had told me cancer was a disease where 'Mummy's cells had gone a bit wrong'. So I asked Sandra if she meant I had killed my mum. She sidestepped my question dismissively. What she meant, she said, 'Was that one possible cause of cancer was stress,' so she couldn't quite confirm it.

I carried the belief that I had killed my mother for several years. Even though somewhere in the depths of my subconscious I knew it wasn't true, it added another layer to my grieving process, a complicated guilty layer. I also didn't know Sandra was making it hard to see my aunties. I thought perhaps they didn't want to see me because they were angry I'd killed Mum. Even writing this now, as a 35-year-old woman who knows very clearly she didn't cause her mother's death, feels hard. I feel like I need to really make a point to tell you it wasn't my fault. The guilt and despair are somehow engrained in me like a faded tattoo that I can't scrub off. I didn't kill Mum. I didn't give her the cancer. It wasn't my fault.

God, I miss her so much. As much as I love this book and love that you are so kindly reading it, I'd rather have her here and no book. I'd give anything to never have to write, 'I didn't give her cancer.' Wow. This is a lot. I've gone off-piste. What a pissy piste this is.

Sandra began to criticise every single thing about me. My hair, my body, the way I talked, walked – everything was fair game to her. She called me chubby and then fat, pointed out how my bum stuck out, calling it an 'African bottom'. (I'm very proud of my lovely bottom now, I can tell you!) When I brushed my hair she scoffed, 'Is that how your mother taught you? Well, she was lazy, dirty, a whore.' I was dumbstruck. I'd never heard anyone use the word 'whore' before but I knew by the way she spat it out that it was bad. At other times, Sandra would refer to me as her best friend and treat me to new clothes or sweets, consolidating my reliance on her. She was grooming me. Encouraging me to be silently complicit in the verbal abuse I was on the end of.

Looking back, I can see how what started as 'mere' mental abuse escalated into something far more harmful, but when I was in the middle of it I was shocked and confused, as if it was somehow unexpected. The vile language against my lovely mum continued and Sandra would say the most awful things and I couldn't retaliate – if I did, she shouted more. She threw a shadow over all the happy memories I was trying to cling on to.

Once, she said she had bumped into an old friend of my mum's and this friend had apparently told Sandra that Mum was a really dirty, filthy person. She asked me if this was true and I'm so ashamed to say I said it was. I said yes because, by this point, I was so terrified of what she would do if I disagreed. In a very twisted way, I wanted to please her. Pleasing her was the best option because when she was pleased, she was nice.

I desperately missed my family, my mum, my old, safe, happy life. I was completely lost in this alien new world of just me and Sandra. She had taken what little self-esteem I had and crushed it under her heel, claiming I made bad choices and she was the only one who knew what was right for me. I believed her. I didn't believe her. I had no idea what to believe or who I was but I knew the best thing was to say nothing.

Anything would set her off. But the shouting wasn't enough for Sandra. After a while of living with us she had escalated to shoving me. Then she introduced the occasional smack for good measure. Whatever way I unloaded the dishwasher would be the wrong way and I would be smacked for it. If she discovered a drawer in my bedroom was untidy she would drag me upstairs, empty everything out, break my things and punish me for being lazy. Or dirty. Or a whore. All the names she levelled at my dead mother were used against me too.

There were constant punishments for 'crimes' I had committed that I know now are not crimes. It is not a crime not to fold your clothes up at night. It is not a crime not to put the lid back on the shampoo bottle. I was grounded for a month for not washing my face 'properly'. I was nine years old. Sometimes, the shouting went on for so long I would wet myself because of the sheer trauma of it all and that would just make her more cross. My body rebelled against the stress, parts of it shut down and I didn't start my periods until I was over 16.

I don't really want to spend much time psychoanalysing Sandra. She obviously had control issues, possible childhood trauma of her own, was jealous of a dead woman so beloved and was quite clearly desperately unhappy. Maybe she had suffered regular humiliation in the past because she was very good at that – it felt like it was her forte. There were charts for my behaviour and she was obsessed with me wearing clean knickers. I had to stand over the laundry basket with her and count out the dirty ones to check that I wasn't lying. If I questioned this behaviour I would be punished. Sometimes she would say the dirty pants were clean ones I had put in the wash just to stay out of trouble and punish me for my 'lies'. It was degrading and a fight I could never win.

The housework was my job and we lived in a big house, so there was a lot of it and many opportunities to do it wrong. I can remember once being dragged from room to room by my hair, scrambling to make my legs work underneath me so that the whole chunk of hair didn't come out. Afterwards I brushed my hair and so much of it would be in the brush, I sat and silently cried. On another occasion I fell over and she kicked me repeatedly til I stood up. My chest was in such pain that I went to my room until it stopped, sitting as silently as I could so I didn't draw any more attention to myself. I spent a lot of time trying to be invisible. I knew which floorboard in my bedroom creaked so I avoided those. I'd hold in going to the toilet so I didn't have to walk out onto the landing. I wanted to be as small and unnoticeable as possible. I wanted to be a tiny speck of nothing and I felt like a tiny speck of nothing. I felt, very much, like nobody cared.

She created issues around food. Mealtimes were intense. Often there would be too much food and Sandra would pile up my plate, telling me to eat until I was crying and sick. Afterwards she would chastise me for being so fat and greedy.

This next bit is horrible. It's all horrible but this bit is even more so, and it is such a vivid memory it has stayed with me since. I was 12, I had what she perceived to be a bad school report, Bs not As. She had gone to my parents' evening alone because Dad was on another trip and I was dreading her return. I always dreaded her return from wherever she had been and would watch the drive, waiting for her car to turn in and the sick feeling descend.

She came back from the parents' evening and ordered me to kneel down on my bedroom floor with my face on the bed, face down onto the duvet. Then she sat on my head. I can't be sure how long this lasted but I remember feeling like I had passed out. Weirdly, it's one of the few details I'm not sure of – I can remember clearly the room layout, the bed, even the duvet cover, but I can't remember how long it lasted. I can't believe I'm even writing this at all, but when you have lived this kind of life, the line between normal and abnormal feels blurry. To me then, it was just another day in hell.

On another occasion, she dragged me out of bed for something I had done 'wrong' and, as she did, my face hit the floor and I got a nasty carpet burn across my top lip. The next day, Dad asked me how I had got the injury and I, looking at Sandra and feeling instantly threatened, said I had fallen out of bed. He and Sandra spent the next week joking about how accident-prone I was and calling me Mrs Hitler. I can't tell you how degrading it feels to be mocked like that. To be laughed at in school and to have your parents call you names.

I wish I could say that these were the only incidents where I was physically hurt by her, but there were others. Writing this chapter has hurt. Remembering these things hurts. Sharing them makes me feel a bit sick and, even though I know I shouldn't, I feel ashamed. I feel embarrassed that this happened to me. I feel embarrassed that I didn't do something – run away, call Childline. I feel embarrassed that I was too afraid. I should have been stronger.

Now, I know what you are thinking, or shouting, at this book. Why didn't I tell my dad? Why didn't he see what was going on? I've spent so many years angry at myself for not just telling someone and fighting for myself. A couple of times I did try to say something. When Dad came home after she smothered me on my bed, I tried to tell him. We were in the car and had just pulled into our garage. Dad asked how my week had been and I cried, saying, 'Not very good.' I said, 'She beat me up.' He couldn't believe it and went to speak to Sandra. She was ready for it though and managed to twist things to her advantage, claiming I was exaggerating, lying and being a silly little girl. She told me if I breathed a word more, she would make my life worse than it already was. I remember her very clearly saying that she just didn't care if she did something 'silly' or if she went to prison, and I believed her. I thought, 'Good God, if you don't care about that then I have no hope.' This woman, I thought, would kill me.

You would think that with all the hair pulling, slapping, hitting, spitting (forgot to add that, she spat at me a lot, mostly in my hair or on my face) and other ways in which Sandra was physical with me, she must have left some bruises or other marks. But as far as I can remember, she didn't. At least, I like to think that if she had, Dad would have seen it and done something about it. But I didn't come through this ordeal with no physical 'reminders': once she kicked me in the legs, and I have broken veins to this day where she kicked me; another time she rammed a key into my arm – I still have a scar there. When I have photoshoots for work I put a little bit of concealer on it and think victoriously, 'Fuck you. Look at me now.' I know that's a bit harsh, but it makes me feel better.

She was so incredibly angry with me all the time and there was nothing I could do about it. I spent hours in my bedroom reading – pure escapism and a sanity saver. I would stay very still when she came upstairs. Sometimes she would come in and drag me out of bed, other times she would ignore me and I would be safe for a while.

During this time in my life, I used to play a game. After each incident I would reset a mental clock in my head back to zero. With each day that passed without another incident, I would move the clock round, one, two, three – to see how many days could I reach before I was hit or hurt again. I don't think I ever made it past five days before I had to reset the clock. I counted a lot back then, I still do. It's a coping mechanism. When she was attacking me, I would go limp and count to 100. Now, if I am feeling anxious or watching something uncomfortable on TV, I realise I am quietly counting my way through it.

The mental abuse included throwing out lots of Mum's things as well as my own stuff but there was constant humiliation too. My rucksack was broken and she refused to let me replace it. I secretly had a proper one at school that I would transfer my books into when I got there without her knowing. It is amazing how many coping mechanisms you develop to keep as safe as possible.

I often had broken glasses and my hair kept coming out so I looked weird and this didn't do me any favours with my peers. I had no friends at school and used to go into the toilets at lunchtime, lock myself in a cubicle and sit there till the bell went. I was never bullied at school in the conventional sense, I was just excluded, considered the sad, weird kid with bad hair. Sandra never gave me a packed lunch and didn't care to buy packed lunch items, so I would either try and make my own (with cold potatoes, sliced up, covered in ketchup and sandwiched between bread) or beg for something from other people's. That didn't endear me either. I wasn't allowed a bra or to shave my legs or underarms because I was a 'whore', despite attending an all-girls school and having absolutely zero social life.

Staff at my school were suspicious. They reached out several times but I was too scared to accept their help. I was even visited once by social services, not at my instigation but by a concerned neighbour, however I told them there was nothing wrong and that I loved Sandra, all the while she looked on benignly. We hid it from everyone. She hid it for obvious reasons and I hid it because

I thought I had to as well. I didn't know then that bullies are cowards.

I went into my teens believing I was a dirty liar because I was constantly told that's what I was. I knew it was wrong and I knew she was bad but I was completely powerless to do anything about it. Until I turned 14 and started to have dangerous thoughts towards Sandra.

I was almost as tall as her, possibly as strong as her and my teenage hormones were raging. For the first time, I could feel the fire in my belly. I was ready to rebel. One day, she called me a bitch. Same old, same old. Except this time, I said, 'I'm not the bitch, you are.' She went absolutely gaga and hit me but inside I was victorious. I kept thinking, 'I did it, I called her a bitch.' I was heady from the thrill of it all – maybe I could fight back.

Every time I thought about running away from home, I got stuck at the part where I had no money and nowhere to run to. Nowhere that would keep me safe from Sandra. I was convinced that when I reached 16, I would have some rights; I could run away to the police station and ask them to rehouse me. I know now it's not that easy but these were the days before Google and I lived in naive hope that I just had to reach 16 and I'd be OK.

I was seeing my aunties again on a very sporadic basis (they didn't give up trying to reach me) but I couldn't tell them what was going on as I had been conditioned not to speak about it. I would beg them to let me stay longer at their houses but couldn't say why I didn't want to go home. My erratic behaviour was dismissed as teen angst. I couldn't take much more of it.

My dad decided to throw a New Year's Eve party and it would be extra special because it was the millennium, the year 2000! I knew I couldn't go into a new era as a victim of this insidious, silent abuse. I made a decision. A big one. It feels really vulnerable typing this out because it's not something I like to think about very much. I'm so far away from the person I was then that it hurts my heart to consider that's where I was. It also hurts me to consider that one day my children might read this. I'm sharing it because I want everyone and anyone to know – you can go to very low places and still bounce back. I want to go back in time and hold young Louise and tell her she's a good egg and this won't be her life forever.

There was a first aid cupboard in the kitchen, above our fridge, full of medicines and tablets. I had no idea how much of it I would need to take to kill myself (remember, no internet access) but I reckoned if I took it all, it would work. Taking my own life was my only way out. I would put my plan into action after the party was over – I didn't want to spoil Dad's big night. New Year's Eve came and we all held hands to sing 'Auld Lang Syne'. My dad turned to hug me and, suddenly, I just broke. I loved Dad and couldn't bear to end my life in secret. I whispered, 'Dad, she hurts me, if you don't fix this, I am going to kill myself.'

When you're at the ebb I was at, you have nothing to lose. I didn't care what conversations this led to (and, as you can imagine, it led to a LOT of questions) and I didn't care about self-preservation or keeping all the secrets she wanted me to. It was either say it all and sort it out or commit suicide – both felt like a win to me.

It was such a relief to say it out loud, to tell him what had been happening behind his back for all those years. The following day, as we were clearing up after the party, Sandra screamed at me for doing something wrong and I said, 'Dad, this is how she has been treating me for years.' It all came tumbling out. He told Sandra it was over and, obviously, since you're reading this book, I didn't end my life. Hurrah!

Wow, that was a lot. I'm just going to melt down a family-size chocolate bar and eat it with a wooden spoon, don't mind me.

We don't dwell on it now, but occasionally Dad will share a memory of something in my childhood that makes him laugh. He remembers it one way and I remember with the added abuse factor. A bit like *The X Factor* but this is a prize nobody wants. LOLs, LOLs and double LOLs.

So, finally, when I was 16, Sandra left and my life began. I could either fall apart from everything I had endured or pick myself up and start over. Well, dear reader, I'll be damned if I don't make lemonade out of lemons so I picked myself right up and took a big hard look at things. I'm a survivor! My initial feelings were of relief at being safe. As psychologist Maslow states in his hierarchy of needs (you see, that university education wasn't wasted), my basic needs of safe shelter were met. Then I experienced joy at being free. I still counted my underwear for a while longer but nobody was about to slap me if the wrong number of pants were in the wash basket. Finally, I felt grateful. Strange, I know, but I am a big believer in having an attitude of gratitude. I was grateful that an unspeakable chapter of my life was over and I could look back on the past eight years knowing it was in the past and I had survived, now any day could be amazing. I had won. I'm still winning.

I was a difficult teen. This was blamed on the fact that teens generally are obnoxious and this is their job but I knew it was for different reasons. I was angry, I was empowered and I was never going to be a victim again. I moved to a sixth-form college where nobody knew me. I wanted to be somewhere I wasn't the weird girl who cried in the toilets. When I started at my new school, to my total surprise, other students wanted to be my friend – it was a revelation! I wasn't a horrible, dirty liar, I was just normal (whatever that is) and people liked me! Suddenly, I was invited to the canteen, to someone's house, to a party, and my whole world opened up!

I needed money to buy the sort of freedom I craved (like bus fares, make-up from Boots, outfits from Mark One and CDs) and my pocket money didn't cover those costs. I decided I'd just have to earn the money myself, so I started a little babysitting business. I made leaflets on my dad's computer and delivered them all around the area. I referred to myself as 'the Local Babysitter' and listed my attributes, including my own transport (bicycle) and being semi-fluent in French. Only semi though, not totally. Hilarious.

I was soon out four nights a week, which suited me as I didn't want to be bored at home, and I was earning up to £400 a month, which was more than enough to fund taxis and drinks for my new-found social life. I also had a Saturday job at a local supermarket, stacking shelves, and worked four hours a week on the till at our local chemist. I loved working and I loved earning my own money. It gave me a sense of control and pride over my own life and I still feel like that now. I'm proud to be independent.

Then Dad met someone new and I did my best to avoid them. The woman tried to make an effort with me but I wasn't falling for that again. 'Look, Laura,' I stated clearly, 'you don't like me and I don't like you but we are going to just have to get on with it, if we have to live together.' Laura looked hurt: 'But I do like you!' she said, shocked at how blunt I'd been. 'OK, Laura,' I sighed, 'you like me and I don't like you. Let's keep out of each other's way.' I couldn't wait to leave home and, to be fair, she probably couldn't wait for me to go away either – poor woman! She ended up staying with my dad for a few years but they didn't work out.

Going to university meant escape and I chose one as far away as possible, in Liverpool. It was another opportunity to reinvent myself. Nobody would know I was the sad girl who was painfully shy and insecure. I could tell them I was really cool and they would believe me. So I did. The first friend I made, Faye, became my friend for life. I was standing outside the lift in our halls, the doors opened and there was Faye. I said, 'Are you a fresher?' and she said 'Yes' and that was that. I made lots more friends and discovered boys and how much they like girls and how much I liked that. I had a great time and, after my second year, I didn't want to go back home for the summer. As soon I was there, Dad and I argued and he couldn't understand my fury.

I was no longer the submissive victim, I was enraged and powerful and didn't want to listen to anyone. Although I loved Dad and he loved me, we'd reached a difficult point where we'd both been through such huge things in our lives that we couldn't see eye to eye, couldn't connect. I was so angry that I'd been put in such a terrible childhood situation that I deeply struggled. We were arguing a lot and I couldn't cope. I still feel on edge if people shout near me. It reminds me of Sandra and what comes after shouting.

I had inherited some money from my lovely gran. One day, I went to the bank, withdrew it all, changed my mobile phone and cancelled the payments my father was making into my bank account. On the day of the awful 7/7 bombings, my friend Faye came and picked me up while Dad was out at work and drove me back to Liverpool, two months early. Later that day, I called him to tell him I had left. He was furious and threatened to cut off my allowance. I said I had already done that. I also said he could not contact me as I had a new number. He had to leave me alone and if he didn't, I would never return home. It was brutal but I felt fantastic.

I had been dating Darcy's dad for a while at this point and he was the opposite to my family experience. He was nice and easy to be with, there was no game playing or need to control. His mum was the same. She was a supportive, good woman who restored my faith in maternal love and is a lovely gran to Darcy. She treated me like a daughter and I have a lot of respect for her. A good woman.

Time is a great healer – it's one of the truest clichés I know. When I returned to Northampton I had a fiancé; I was in love and felt loved. I was ready to build bridges with my dad. Anger is a hot stone and by holding it in your hand, you only burn yourself. I had to learn to let go of it. My dad is a good man who made some poor choices which had a detrimental effect on me. We have been to counselling together and talked about this so it will be no surprise to him that I write that. To take the positive view of this, it made me who I am today and how I consider the choices I make for my children. I am extremely vigilant and monitor any changes in their behaviour. I am not paranoid, just aware, and I'm glad to have that skill set in my motherhood pack of cards.

I know you might be wondering what happened to Sandra. I could say she spontaneously combusted into a ball of wicked flames. Or she was locked in a very high tower for all eternity. Or she saw the error of her ways, begged forgiveness and lived out her days volunteering in an orphanage. OK, maybe not an orphanage, a donkey sanctuary perhaps. None of these are true, more's the pity. I didn't see her for a very long time. She carried on with her life and I carried on with mine. I went to college, university, found a boyfriend who became my fiancé, bought a house, married, had a baby and became a mother.

The Sandra wounds were healing. Sometime after Darcy's dad and I split, he met somebody else and one day, he told me he was going to introduce Darcy to his new girlfriend that afternoon. I freaked out. I had one of the few panic attacks I have ever had. It was so bad I thought it was a heart attack and nearly rang an ambulance. Logically, I knew Darcy was not in danger but I couldn't shake the fear that what had happened to me would happen to her too.

Later that week, I was in the car, driving down a steep hill with a sharp turn at the bottom. I thought, 'What if I don't turn the wheel? What if I just drive straight into the wall, crash the car and die? I could and that would stop this pain that has bubbled back up.' It wasn't pre-meditated, it just popped into my head, and as soon as it did, I thought about my beautiful three-year-old daughter and how I could never do that to her. She was more than enough reason to live.

I went straight home, googled local counsellors and booked in. On my first session, I turned up and said (I'm summarising an entire hour here), 'Hello, I think I have been abused and now I am afraid my daughter will be.' I was reassured that these thoughts were perfectly valid and that I was projecting my own experiences and I could learn how to deal with these debilitating thoughts. Let me share two tips that I still use regularly:

1. If a bad memory is haunting you, drain all the colour out of it. If you do have to remember it then do so in black and white. It takes the pain out a bit. Only good memories deserve technicolor.

2. If a person is haunting you, if you keep seeing their face in your mind's eye, then picture yourself blowing them down a long tunnel, far into the distance out of sight. Byyyyeeee!

So, where was I? Using delaying tactics to answer your question about whatever happened to Sandra, that's where. I have seen her twice since she left. The first time was several years ago. I was in a park with Darcy and she came over to say hello, overly friendly, suggesting we meet up for coffee. I stood there thinking, 'What the hell are you talking about?' I took my courage in both hands and said, 'Sandra, after what you did to me, I don't ever want to see you again.' Brazenly, she denied it all, had no idea what I was talking about and said I must have imagined it. That was the end of that, until early 2019. This is going to surprise you. I mean, it rather surprised me!

I had made a New Year's resolution to find peace in all areas of my life. Shortly after, I was driving past where I knew Sandra lived and a spark of an idea pinged into my mind. What if I found peace here too? Could I actually just go and do that? I could try! I knew her house and I found myself pulling up outside it. Was I really going to be able to confront her? I told myself I was a weighty 33-year-old who could probably throw a hefty punch if I needed to. I knocked on the door and she answered. I told her I was looking to find some peace and she – rather shocked, I think – invited me in. Finally I was able to tell her how I truly felt. And I did. I told her that I knew what she did to me. That it was wrong.

I remember that moment so clearly. It was a small moment that felt massive. To have the opportunity to tell someone like that how you see them – it's powerful. She didn't confirm or deny it but said she was happy to sit down and talk about it further, to explain things. Maybe she'd admit it or maybe she'd twist it like before, but I don't think there is any explanation for what happened and I had said what I needed to say. I had made her face me and maybe, in the quiet of her mind, face what she did. So I just walked away.

Hilariously, I actually had to do the school pick up, which I did, came home, cooked fish fingers and watched *Peppa Pig* with the girls, so I didn't actually have a moment to feel really incredible or soak it up. It had been a momentous day but my normal life trundled along past it. Classic mum life.

So what happens next? It may surprise you to hear this, but I have forgiven her. Not for her, but for me. Hate is a strong emotion and I don't want to expend any more energy on her; she is not worth my rage and it doesn't do me or my children any good to hold on to it. I don't speak of the sort of spiritual forgiveness where the slate is wiped clean and the perpetrator embraced. It's the acceptance that this happened to me, it's over, I don't need to give it any more oxygen and **I have won**. My only regret is that I didn't call Childline. I know they would have been a listening ear and a lifeline. They may have given me the confidence to speak out sooner. It's why I am now a supporter of the charity and promote all the brilliant work they do. It's very healing too.

I deliberated over whether to include Sandra in this story and how much I should say. I think it is important that I have, as hard as it is to write – and I know it's not much fun to read. I questioned whether she even deserved to be part of this memoir because I wouldn't say there was a maternal bond or any kind of positive motherly standards met, but sadly, I know I'm not alone and that this isn't a unique experience to just me. Sandra assumed a maternal role in my life and she was a bad egg, rotten actually. This is my history but it isn't my future. I feel safe and strong, I have a lovely life and I am grateful for the person I am today, however I was shaped.

So, like I said, not many LOL LOL LOL moments in this chapter, my friends. I think it is fitting to end this section like they do over the credits of a TV programme that has depicted hard-hitting themes. In my best 'snazzy telly voice' I would like to say, if you have been affected by any of the issues shared here please do contact the marvellous people below . . .

Childline: 0800 1111, www.childline.org.uk
NAPAC (National Association for People Abused in Childhood): 0808 801 0331, www.napac.org.uk
NSPCC (National Society for the Prevention of Cruelty to Children): 0808 800 5000, www.nspcc.org.uk
Samaritans: 116 123, www.samaritans.org
Women's Aid: www.womensaid.org.uk

# Chapter 8

# My Rebel Girls

OK, so how do we follow a chapter like that?! With a list of amazing, incredible, brilliant women, THAT'S HOW! Through the course of my career, I have been incredibly lucky, attending or taking part in the most amazing events, campaigns and charities. When the UN gave me a call in 2015, I was completely speechless. There I was, pootling about my little house in Northampton, making videos for a bunch of nice gals online and – ta da! – the United freakin' Nations are on the phone! They were looking for ambassadors for their Global Goals campaign and wanted to know if I was interested in being a part of it. It was an overwhelming privilege to be included. Even more so, as, out of the listed 17 goals that they wanted to focus on, including no poverty, zero hunger, quality education and clean water, they had asked me to be part of number five, gender equality. I was the European envoy, invited to join a selection of women from around the world to meet in New York and discuss the messages that needed to be shared.

This experience and my involvement in empowering other women changed me in two ways. It gave me a much better awareness of the work we still need to do around gender equality globally. Second to that, it reminded me of the responsibility I have as a mother of two girls to bring them up knowing they are equal.

Darcy and I talk a lot about this and I will do the same with Pearl when she is older. I plan on it being an ongoing conversation in our household. I bought Darcy the book *Good Night Stories for Rebel Girls* and she loves it. We read it together and talk about all the amazing women we find between the pages. Learning more about these strong, incredible women who have changed the world is the best inspiration. They are the role models I choose for my girls. It makes me think about who I would include in my own book of influential women, those who have inspired, encouraged or touched my life in some way.

Of all the marvellous women in my family, it goes without saying that my mum is the best egg of all. In my eyes, she's an absolute queen and everything I aim to be, but for now, we'll let some of the other wonderful women in my life shine.

My grannies are definitely top of my Rebel Girls list. Granny Gill, my mum's mum, was my original single mum role model. She divorced my grandad (he was a VERY bad egg) in the 1960s and held her head high through the stigma, working full-time and raising three girls with love and fortitude. She did her absolute best at all times and for that I give her the title of the Ultimate Mighty Mum.

Dad's mum, Grandma Peggy Pentland, is still with us, the epitome of grace and dignity. She stepped in with kindness and care when Mum was ill and became my safety net when Mum was dying. She's given me so much guidance and advice throughout my life. She taught me that a lady should always have £40 cash on her because that's enough to sort out most emergency situations. She taught me how to sew a button onto a shirt, how to iron (not something I do very much but if I want to, thanks to her, I can, haha!) and she has shown me what self-respect looks like. At 96, she still carries herself with total assurance.

When my stepmother Tina came into my life, about ten years ago now, the sun shone on our family again. Tina is a woman who loves relentlessly and selflessly, she stepped into my broken family and, like glue, stuck us all back together again. I've always been close with my mum's side but it's been different with Dad's side. I think because we'd been through so very much, we'd learnt to survive but not to live. We'd stopped doing things like family parties or meals out together but Tina brought all those back with joy. Her unfailing support has had a huge impact on my life.

Tina was the first person I left my first baby with, which any mother will know is a Big Moment. Darcy was born on 6th April and my birthday is 28th April. I'd been at home for three weeks with my newborn bundle and, as you know, it'd been a bit of a rough start. I can't remember who suggested I should go out for my birthday (not 'out out', just out to the cinema – a short car journey and nice sit down were about all I could muster!) but I was horrified at the idea. I couldn't fathom that it would be alright to leave my baby but Tina insisted it would be OK and she wanted to do it. Nervously, I accepted the help and Tina came and took charge – she didn't even look offended when I handed her two A4 sheets of paper with 'Darcy's Notes' on, haha!

I had three hours out of the house and felt amazing for it. I'm glad she pushed me to do that and I'm glad of all the subsequent support she's offered too. She picked up Darcy from nursery in the early days when I was growing my business and having to go to London; she's taken care of my cats (despite not loving the litter tray duties!) when I took Darcy on our first 'Mummy and me' holiday and she continues to let me moan down the phone to her whenever I need to. She has been the very best type of big-hearted stepmother and I would have been proud to have her as a mum.

It's difficult to single out one friend among the lovely ones I have, but if we are talking about Warrior Women then the accolade has to go to my good friend Clare. She had a difficult journey to pregnancy and when she did finally conceive, she was diagnosed with gestational diabetes. The tough time continued with a traumatic delivery of her daughter and an even tougher time breastfeeding. But, being the most positive person in the world that she is, Clare carried on with a smile on her face and an attitude of gratitude like I've never seen before. I never heard her complain or moan. She accepted it was hard and carried on loving and laughing. And, after all that, she did it again! Her next gorgeous baby took a long time to come along but, once more, Clare (and her lovely husband) stayed positive. Whenever I'm having a hard mummy day I think, 'What would Clare do now?' and I'm instantly motivated to keep going. Love you, Clare.

When I think of someone who has made a blended family bloom, I think of my glorious friend Esther. She has three children, one from her first marriage and two more with her lovely husband, Raj. Esther was there when I was single and lost. She reminded me time and time again that families come in all sizes and they can all work. She's guided, loved and supported. She's come along on some absolutely mad adventures (#TheHorses), joined the PTA with me (the discos we organised in the school hall when we were living our ultimate MumLife will stay with me forever), she reminds me to take things off my shoulders and she never, ever judges. Ever. Esther is a sister of my soul and a mum I hold in the highest regard. She's a bit of legend, actually.

In the vlogging world, I have met some incredible women who have developed from colleagues into friends. One of them is Carrie Hope Fletcher, a vlogger, author and performer who is one of those all-round talents. She's no doubt impressive but what truly inspires me is her energy. She takes life by the horns and runs with it! I actually think she literally runs marathons too, but that's not the talent I meant with the horn-running, LOL. I love a woman who lives her life like this – I love a 'doer'.

Very similar is my manager Meghan, who I have renamed Meghan the Machine. Every day she astounds me with how smart she is and how she can find a solution to any problem – and I've thrown a variety at her, let me tell you! It scares me that she is this wise and still in her mid-twenties. Her guidance and safe pair of hands makes it easier for me to stride out into my career and continually challenge myself. Her never-ending support makes it easier for me to stride out into my life. She's far more than just a manager to me. (Incredibly awkward though if she reads this and doesn't feel the same. . .)

This chapter is at risk of turning into something more appropriate for the acknowledgements page so I am going to chuck in a few of my fave famous women too.

I am a huge royalist and a big fan of the Queen particularly, but I am going to give the honour to HRH Camilla, Duchess of Cornwall. The main reason for choosing her, apart from her hard work and dedication to the job of right-hand woman, is because of the work she does with Bookstart, part of the Book Trust, which encourages childhood literacy. I met Charles and Camilla when they came into the YouTube offices. Camilla is patron of the charity and wanted to meet creators who also supported them. I was invited to join them and loved chatting to Camilla about the work the charity is doing, what she likes to read and my life as an author. I sent her my books afterwards, because who doesn't need a bit of Robin Wilde in their lives? I received the loveliest thank you letter in return.

Moving on from one amazing lady to another, Emma Freud. Author, presenter, co-founder and director of Comic Relief. I am forever impressed by her. She just does SO much, works incredibly hard, looks after her large family and does it with joyful vigour and humour (and I am not just saying this because I love Badger, her cat). I have had the pleasure of hanging out at her house, joining her family for dinner and, when I was feeling lost and sad in New York, popping round to their apartment for a much-needed hug. I even made a tiny appearance in the Comic Relief follow-up to *Love Actually*, so at least I can say I have been in a film. Sort of.

I don't kid myself that just because of the charity work I do and my UN ambassador role that I am able to change the world, but I do believe we should all be braver about using our voice and doing what we can. I am proud of the work I have done but I know there is so much more to do, which is why I am including Greta Thunberg on my Rebel Girls list. I am bowled over by her commitment to what matters and how simple and strong her message is.

I also hugely admire the barrister Amal Clooney, who specialises in human rights as well as being the special envoy on media freedom. She is also married to the silver fox, George Clooney, but that is just an aside. I hugely admire her academic brain and commitment to international law and charity. I can't say I have met her but we were in the same room once . . . It was the strangest day all round, because it started with an audience with the Pope. Yes, you heard me.

The Vatican rang one day and asked if I wanted to come to Rome to meet the Pope as he was keen to spread a message of peace and love to younger people. I took my dad with me and we sat with the Pope in a small room and chatted for an hour with the help of translators. As I left, he gave me some rosary beads and asked me to join him at a charity awards ceremony that was taking part in another section of the Vatican. I risked missing my plane home but I couldn't refuse the Pope, so I popped along for the first part, following George Clooney down the corridor and joining him, Amal and Richard Gere. When I was sat on the plane waiting to take off back to the UK, my dad and I kept shaking our heads in amazement. What a day!

I could continue talking about all the brilliant women I have been influenced by in one way or another but this book just isn't long enough. Another time maybe, over a cuppa or a bottle of fizz. Including the women I have makes me realise that we should be thankful for those around us every day. And give a rebel yell!

# Chapter 9

# Working Motherhood

Embarking on motherhood is hard enough without throwing in additional pitfalls to the journey, like needing to find a job and pay your bills. The truth is that many of us can't afford not to work and it's also true that some of us want to work, whatever our financial situation. It is also undeniable that giving up work and being a stay-at-home parent is the hardest job of all.

If I was PM for the day (and yes, I know, I would be amazing), the first law I would pass would be annual leave for stay-at-home parents. Their job combines parenting with being a cleaner, chauffeur, chef, first aider, mediator and teacher – they deserve a break at the end of all that! It is amazing and exhausting all rolled into one. You can feel every emotion in a single day and still go back for more. It is both a privilege but often thankless, it can be mind-numbingly boring and magically wonderful. I am in awe of any mum (or dad) who makes the choice to stay at home – you have magic powers!

My life as a working mother started from financial necessity. This is still the case but now with the bonus that I do a job I love, which often enhances my quality of life – I know how lucky I am to have this. Back when I fell pregnant with Darcy, I was working in an office as PA to a manager. The manager left and wasn't replaced, which made my job hard, being a personal assistant to someone who no longer existed. Sadly, I wasn't on a permanent job contract so I didn't qualify for anything more than the statutory maternity pay from the government which, at the time, was around £400 a month. This was a big step down from the roughly £1,400 a month I'd been bringing in before and so we had to cut our cloth accordingly. I didn't buy all the latest gadgets and gizmos for Darcy's arrival, but do you know what? It was fine. Now that I've lived both ways (having the basics for Darcy and all the frills for Pearl), I can honestly say that even though the extras are nice, I don't think they made anyone vastly happier. Easier yes, happier, I'm not sure.

I knew we couldn't sustain this way of life for too long as the maternity pay didn't last forever and we wanted to build a future, so going back to the office was always on the cards. But I was dreading returning to my old job (I'd planned to find another office that had a vacancy) as I had no security there or passion for what I was doing. Also, I think it would be fair to say I was absolutely terrible at office admin roles. Organisation and logistics are not my strong suit – but I was fast learning that online communication was.

The blog I'd started in September 2009 became a creative lifeline. It gave me something to focus on during those long days at home with a newborn and I was finding the digital community a really friendly place to be. The problem was, it was just a hobby. I remember talking to a friend and saying, 'It's a really lovely thing to do but you've got to have your heart in it because it's not a money thing. You just do it for the love of it.' That same friend pointed out that a lot of websites sold little bits of space to advertisers and I wondered if I could do the same. I was clueless but I had nothing to lose and the end of maternity leave was looming. I sold my first bit of ad space for £50. A company 'rented' a long rectangle across the top of my blog for one month and I was thrilled! I couldn't bloody believe it! Suddenly all sorts of things seemed possible.

I worked hard on my blog and was repaid in followers and interest from the online community. I respected it like a proper job, researching the industry to work out what was successful, uploading regularly, understanding SEO (search engine optimization) and digital trends. I worked harder than I ever had done in my office roles and felt more fulfilled from the fledgling career than I ever anticipated

I would. I knew if I could earn a basic salary of £400 a month (roughly to match my maternity pay that we had managed on so far) without needing to leave Darcy and the house then I had cracked it. It wasn't a business, it was a side hustle, a chance to earn a bit of cash to contribute to monthly living expenses. I never expected it to develop further. Every evening I would work on my master plan till late and the following day, during Darcy's naps, I would put it into practice in any scraps of time I had.

Vlogging was the natural next step and I took it, making one-take-wonder videos on my fuzzy webcam and uploading them straight onto YouTube. I wasn't constrained by editing, filters, brand awareness or people's expectations, it was very simple. It isn't now, it's a much harder industry to crack these days – I was lucky that I was there at the start.

Darcy was the easiest toddler ever and I could work a little when she was around, but I was starting to need to work a bit more than before. I was earning enough to pay for some help so I found a lovely local nursery and signed her up for two days a week. She loved it and I loved having a bit of time to myself. Nursery combined with my stepmother Tina was a godsend. I could get so much more done with my business and this was quickly reflected in the revenue it was bringing in and the management company now looking after me.

What I didn't do was talk about this support system online. I had complicated feelings of guilt that I had made this decision. I could afford childcare, I had a husband and family support and, because of that, I never talked about how much I needed that help and how much I benefited from it. Not just financially, because I could do more work, but mentally and emotionally too. I was able to have a bit of space to myself (again, I feel a bit guilty for suggesting I wanted to be away from my baby sometimes even though that's so OK), I had a project of my own to focus on that didn't revolve around taking care of other people (hi, yes, feel guilty for saying that too) and – guess what else? Sometimes I didn't do a day of work. Sometimes I'd just enjoy the quiet or see a friend or catch up on TV shows I enjoyed! There! I've said it! I feel equally liberated and terrified of being judged!

Jokes aside, if I could turn the clock back and retain the confidence in myself that I have now, I would have been much more upfront. I feel like I was doing such a disservice to those women who were watching my vlog and asking themselves, 'I don't know how she does it!' 'With help!' I should have said. 'With a lot of flipping help!'

When I had Pearl, I thought it would be just as easy as when Darcy was a baby. I assumed that, for the first couple of years, I'd manage to work around her, in naptimes and at night, and then I'd look at nursery help. Well, within a month it was evident that this was not the case and I felt ridiculous for even thinking I could have managed like that. I'd not taken into account the fact I wasn't writing a low-traffic hobby blog anymore, I'd built a successful business which had lots of facets to it and needed a lot of my input.

A few people suggested I take proper maternity leave but I didn't feel like I could. Social media is a funny fish and at the risk of sounding like a total knob (if I haven't already, haha!), if I take six months off, nobody else can step in and be 'me' in the meantime. I had Pearl on a Sunday and was back at the laptop on Monday. I love what I do, so I am not complaining, but I am also the breadwinner responsible for the mortgage and school fees so I can't stop for longer than a couple of weeks' holiday. A successful, multi-layered business employing a team of people can't just be run in nap times.

At first, I tried to make it work. I'd wave Liam off to work in the mornings, set Pearl up for her breakfast bottle, wind her, change her, settle her and then she'd nap. While she was asleep, I'd plan to sort myself out and do some work but by the time I'd had a shower and tidied up from breakfast, she'd be awake and we'd start again. I'd lay her down for another little nap, do ten minutes of work and then I'd have to put her in the car to collect Darcy from school. Then I'd help with homework, give Pearl an afternoon bottle, sort out some dinner and Liam would come home. I was also doing all the normal life admin and family running and I was feeling VERY tired. Most days I'd end up in tears because I was so cross I couldn't squeeze it all in. Even if Liam took over everything the second he came home, I still couldn't do it. Surprise, surprise, I wasn't actually the Superwoman I thought I was. That Superwoman doesn't exist.

I started looking at local nurseries but Pearl was just so young and I couldn't bear to leave her. A vlogger friend mentioned employing a nanny as an option. I remember thinking that sounded so weird. People like the royal family hire nannies, not somebody like me in a house in Northampton, earning a living from a YouTube channel, sharing my passions for Disney, charity shops and pink hair. I didn't think I was the type to have a nanny. I thought all nannies were either Mary Poppins or the ones you see in beige uniforms pushing the big old-fashioned Silver Cross prams at royal christenings. But my friend said having a nanny had been a 'game changer' and I knew I needed to change the bloody game I was trying to play. This friend of mine was very normal, there is nothing regal about her at all (she'll love that!), so if she had one, maybe I should think about it, maybe it wasn't such an outlandish idea. She recommended me to an agency, I trusted her judgement and, after further research, I met them, explained what I wanted and began an interview process.

It is the strangest feeling to be interviewing someone to step into your role. It felt disloyal, like I was ready to hand my children over and relinquish my job as Mum. Except that wasn't what happened at all. I learnt so much about my maternal self and I felt utter relief that I had the support when I was working and could be completely dedicated to my children when I was not. I no longer had to live in that half-working, half-childcare twilight when you aren't doing either thing properly and you just feel more and more cross with yourself. The juggle struggle became less of a juggle and less of a struggle. We found a routine and system that we all liked and I'm so happy I took this leap. I hired the nanny for four days a week so I still had a day midweek to be with Pearl and, of course, every weekend. If you can (and I do appreciate it's not on the cards for everyone), it's OK to seek help.

The weekday I have with Pearl is incredibly special and I fiercely protect it. She and I go to the park, to toddler groups or baby ballet, to the supermarket and live a normal life without me being harassed (I mean by my tasks and to-do lists, not by actual people!), too tired to play with her or escaping to my laptop while her back is turned. We take Darcy to and from school, organise playdates and make time for lots of snuggles.

On my working days, the nanny arrives at 8am and takes over just as the girls are finishing breakfast. She takes Pearl out to baby groups and meets up with the brilliant network of local nannies (turns out more people than you think have nannies!) who plan fun day trips and adventures. My children are looked after by an experienced, strong, funny woman who cares deeply for them and I couldn't be more pleased and grateful for what she gives me. I really do appreciate that this is a privilege not always possible for others. That would be my second priority as PM, to offer more affordable childcare and flexible options. My manifesto is coming together nicely . . .

I feel it is my duty to tell you this and be as honest as possible, because if you don't tell other women your secrets, they think you are smashing it. They want to know how you can run a successful business, bring up happy children, maintain a loving adult relationship and still be smiling at the end of the day. I am only smashing it (truthfully, not always smashing it actually, sometimes just blindly winging it) because of the team of amazing women

I have that support me in all areas of my life. I can't stress enough how I don't do any of this alone.

I interviewed the fabulously witty TV presenter Angela Scanlon for a podcast recently. She said people used to ask her if she had a nanny and she would mumble and say she had 'someone who helped' but she realised she was letting other women down by not being honest. There is no shame in having help. Only a couple of generations before us, people would live near their families, stay in their communities and be supported by parents and extended family members. As I often like to say, it takes a village to bring up a child. With the addendum that you can create that village if it doesn't already exist.

Being honest about employing a nanny has been a gift to the online naysayers. The phrase 'you can't please 'em all' has never been more apt. I've been called 'lazy', a 'part-time mum' and much worse, but I'm not going to use the pages of my own book to write other people's insults in it. When they take the time to write their own books and have them published, they can write them themselves, eh? Teehee!

There is nothing noble in struggling when you can see a better path and you are able to take it. I remind myself that I'm living my life for my family and not to try to appease a very small portion of people that are unkind. The majority of my audience have been so lovely and so supportive, I really value them. I think though, different opinions are all part of the job. If you ask people to watch your videos, buy your books, follow you on social media and yet tell them not to have an opinion, it seems a little unfair. I've learnt to take it on the chin, listen to it all, decide what I think is best for my own children and our own family, and carry on. I think you'd call that 'growing very thick skin'.

Most working mothers don't take their children to work with them. My children are a small part of my work and involving them is tricky. I have chosen this job, they haven't, so I am constantly looking at restrictions around what they do. We have a lot of family rules about what we will and won't film, though I don't tend to talk about them publicly because I feel like our boundaries are private choices, but they centre around security, dignity and the future.

Most of our family trips and experiences aren't filmed (I feel so torn on that because I love watching back the trips I do vlog, but I also want the children to remember me being present) and I don't tend to whip out my camera in a packed playground, at school or in our immediate local area. Sometimes I'm accused of filming 'everything' which simply isn't true. I was interviewed recently and asked,

'Why would you share every detail of your life?' 'I don't,' I answered, 'I share no more than 30 per cent of it, but if you think I am sharing everything then I am doing a really good job!'

Darcy loves being in front of the camera. I regularly go to edit and find she's filmed little clips when I wasn't there! They don't go into the vlogs but I enjoy them and save them for us. Despite this, and even though there are so many lovely things to film, I try to make compassionate choices about when we do and don't put ourselves 'out there'. It's important to me that Darcy and Pearl have a big portion of their lives offline and have their childhoods protected. I don't judge anyone for how much they do or don't share online, I think it's a really personal and ever-evolving choice.

I'm sometimes asked if I'd like Darcy or Pearl to follow in my footsteps and do what I do. I always answer the same – 'Yes, I'd like them to find a job they love and look forward to doing every day, I'm not too fussed if that's vlogging or writing or anything else.' I'm proud of my career and proud of myself for working my not-so-little butt off and finding ways to be a mummy and have the best job in the world. I hope that helps inspire them to run at life and achieve their wildest dreams.

Something I am particularly proud of being is an author. Even if it's a part of my business that I love and hate in equal measure! Before this book, I have written three novels and one non-fiction book. Every time I write a book I go in with blind optimism and excitement leading to a small but noticeable breakdown as I get close to deadline. It's an incredibly stressful and totally addictive experience! I spend half the year hating the writing process and the other half of the year skipping around announcing I have written a book. The end result is always worth it. It's exactly like pregnancy and labour – I forget the agony and then decide to do it all again.

I could write a book on how to write a book, including:

1. How to ignore emails your agent and editor send, politely checking 'How are you getting on?'

2. How to procrastinate – my house has never been as clean as when I am on deadline.

3. How to bend the truth and tell your editor you have written more words than you may actually have. 'Yep, I think we're nearing the halfway point.' ARGH!

4. How to celebrate once the book is out there. That's the best part!

My Robin Wilde trilogy is close to my heart. I am often asked if the character and story are based on me and my life. The first book, *Wilde Like Me*, tells the story of a semi-glamorous 29-year-old woman with a five-year-old daughter. Vaguely familiar?! There are some parallels but as the story has developed and became a second book, *Wilde About the Girl*, and then a third, *Wilde Women*, the characters have taken on a life of their own. The main character, Robin, struggles with the challenges of motherhood and I would have found that difficult to write without delving deep into my own experiences. You don't know loneliness until you are a single mum, sitting in the bath drinking Disaronno and Coke out of a plastic Peppa Pig cup, scrolling through a list of Tinder rejects on your phone.

This leads me nicely into feeling overwhelmed. I have a really 'fun' habit of thinking I have more time than I do, taking on more projects than I can manage, missing all the deadlines, having a big cry and promising myself I'll be more sensible next time. It's inevitable that we will all feel like this and this is when we must remember to stop and step back. I have been bad at doing that in the past.

In December 2015, I hit a real low patch, I couldn't cope, I had taken too much on and had nobody to blame but myself, which made it worse. I called my manager and sobbed down the phone. It was hard to admit I was struggling and needed help. I cancelled everything that month; I lost work, money and evenings out, but I gained time, my sanity and a lot more cuddles with Darcy. Had I stopped earlier, when the warning signs were there and taken a few days off, I wouldn't have crashed so spectacularly later. So now I make sure those I work with know it is OK for them to do just that. A self-care afternoon, a down day, call it what you will, sometimes makes all the difference.

This chapter has been about my personal experience as a working mother. It is not an essay on working motherhood or an in-depth analysis based on talking to 100 women from different backgrounds and careers. It is just my story. With one big message to take away from it if you can – DO WHAT YOU NEED TO DO. I know exactly how it feels to hear other people's opinions about parenting, life choices, hairstyles and #mumlife without you asking for it. Ignore it all and make decisions based on what is right for you and your family.

## How to Be a Working Mother (in my VERY humble opinion)

1. *Ignore Mum guilt with a firm hand and remember who you are doing this for. It is hard enough to keep the juggling act going without being weighed down with the guilt of a thousand perceived failings. You may not do every school run and you might dash in late for parents' evening – it happens. Equally, there are times when you need to put those things first and delay work. I delayed a whole book tour once so I could be at Darcy's sports day. I knew that wasn't the BEST career choice but it was the BEST choice for the bigger life picture.*

2. *If you are happy working and love what you do, you will be a happier mummy. It is good for your children to see this. It is also important that they know it's not always easy.*

3. *I have said it before and I am going to say it again: remember, it takes a village to raise a child. Accept help, involve grandparents if they are around, find a good local nursery or childminder. Swap favours with other parents. Both my girls loved toddler groups and*

*Darcy was so happy at nursery. It has made them more sociable, relaxed and curious to be in another world.*

4. *Calendar management is key. Children teach you that you can survive on less sleep than you think and be more organised than you knew possible. I cannot function without an online calendar, synched with Liam's and shared with my team.*

5. *You are not playing second fiddle to your partner's job just because you are the woman. There should be a mutual respect and if there isn't then something needs to change.*

6. *Streamline your domestic life. If you can, hire a weekly cleaner (a luxury to many I know but worth the £20 a week, if feasible) or do your food shop online. One of my neighbours has all her washing collected each week and then it's returned ironed – she's a genius!*

7. *Sacrifices will be made. You have to be OK with that. It isn't possible to do it all so something will have to give. In my life, it is watching lots of TV (which I find frustrating as there is so much good drama*

I have missed over the years) and exercise (which is not much of a sacrifice for me, let's be honest).

8. Treat yourself and your family regularly. You are working hard, you deserve something back and a moment to hop off the relentless working mother wheel. It can be as simple as taking them out to the park for some special mummy time or maybe it's a full-on adventure away. Think about you too. Have you had your eye on that novelty cat-shaped velvet handbag with gold stitching? Treat yo'self, I won't judge you!

Mum, Dad and I. Happiest times.

Grandma Peggy (*above*) and Grandma Jill (*left*).

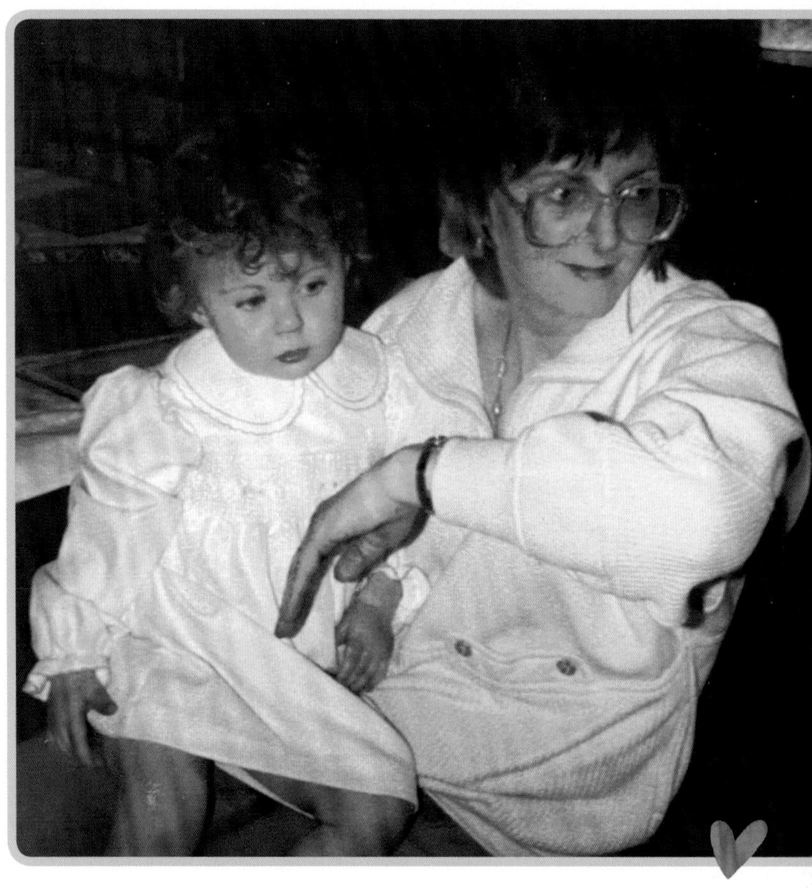

My gorgeous mum, gone but never forgotten.

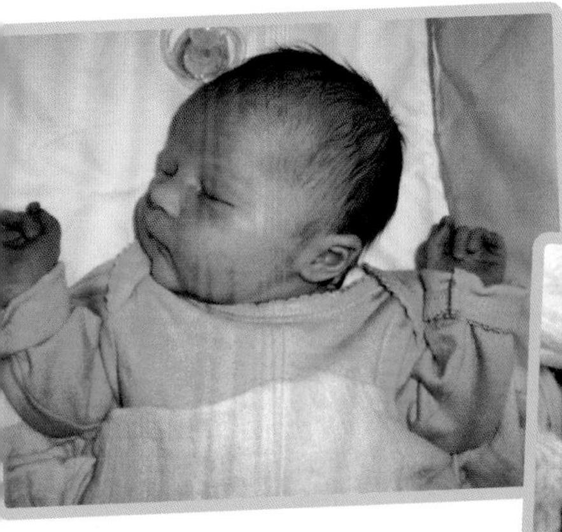

Baby Darcy – the one that made me a mummy, Darcy Jane.

Grown Darcy – now a big girl, making me proud every single day.

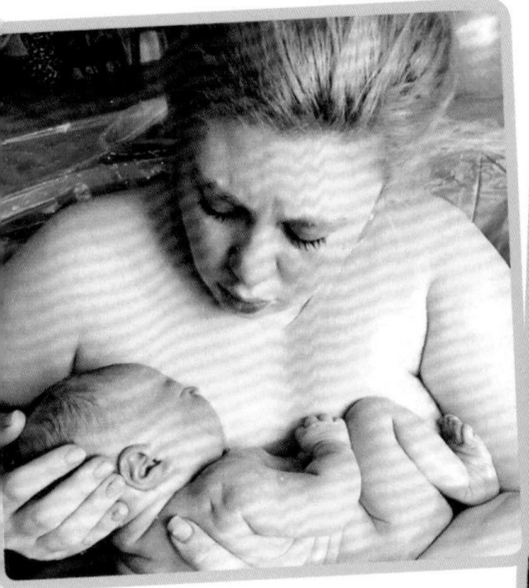

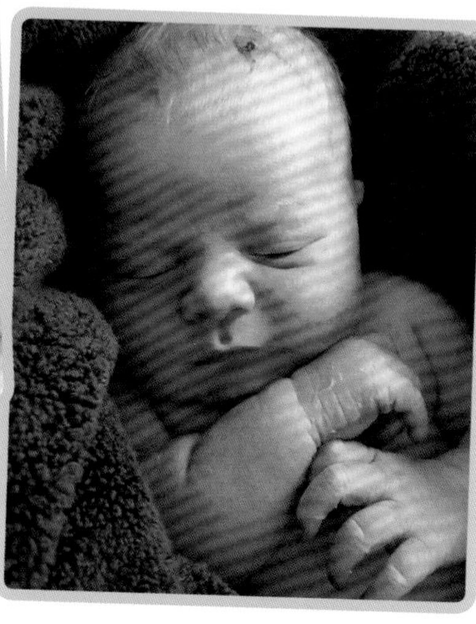

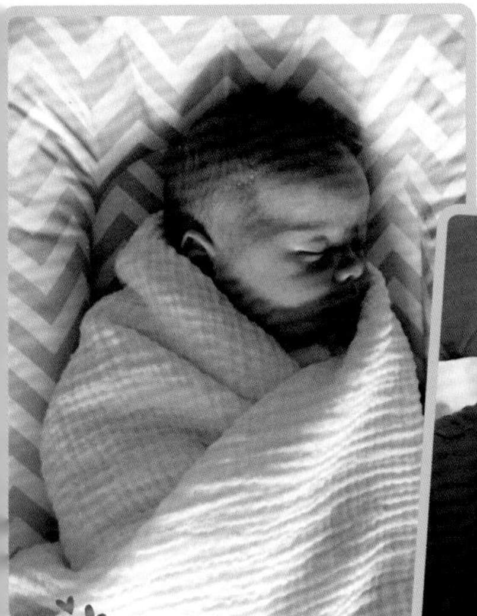

Welcome to the world, Pearl Jane – my little Pearliepops!

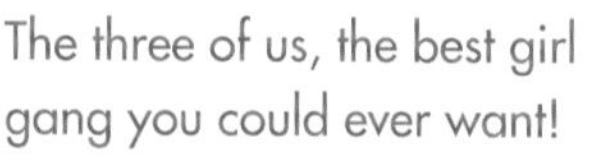

The three of us, the best girl gang you could ever want!

#MumLife

The Good Man! Hurrah for finding him!

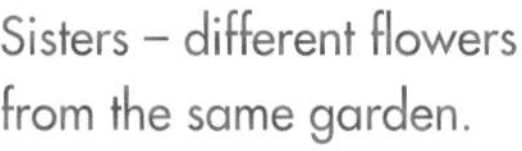

Sisters – different flowers from the same garden.

# Chapter 10

# Bodies & Boobies

You know me (or if you didn't then I am hoping you do by this point!), I call a spade a spade. I love my body, it housed my babies and gave me the most beautiful gifts I could have ever wanted, but I'm pretty realistic about it. My boobies are less bouncy-roundy and more puffy-pitta-pockets; I call that under-part of my tummy (sad times that I have an 'under-part') 'the jibble' and I don't think I'll be winning any trampolining competitions any time soon, because two 9lb+ babies later and that pelvic floor isn't quite as strong as it once was! (Don't lie, did you just do a little pelvic squeeze to see if you still could? Every time I read this paragraph back, I do!) Over the past ten years, my relationship with my body has had good and bad times and I'd imagine you're pretty similar.

As I mentioned earlier, when Darcy was born, I thought I would breastfeed her. I didn't think very hard about it, I just assumed I would. The women in the 'Breast is Best' posters at the doctors looked so happy and smiley – I thought they looked like Proper Mothers and that was what I wanted to be.

At the back of my mind, I think I believed that if I fed my baby any other way, or even considered it, I wouldn't have been doing it 'right' and I would absolutely not be a Proper Mother.

Someone I knew who had successfully breastfed once said dismissively, 'Those women who struggled just weren't trying hard enough,' and that haunted me for years. I thought that if I found it difficult, it was just because I wasn't trying enough. So, I kept trying to breastfeed Darcy. I really, really tried. With the result that she had lost more weight than normal (a lot of babies lose a little bit of weight after they are born) and the midwife told us to take her to hospital immediately to be checked over.

I was distraught, in pain, struggling with undiagnosed PTSD and my body was still not my own. When we went to the hospital, we established that my breasts weren't giving her enough milk. Maybe this was due to the vast amount of blood I lost in childbirth, maybe it was something else, we never really tested, but I felt like I hadn't done my best and that I'd let her down. We went away to our little hospital room and for the next two days she was bottle-fed and loved it. I started to have a bit more sleep, we found a routine, she gained weight, it was amazing. After that, we decided to exclusively bottle feed and it was the right choice for us.

I want to be very clear and say that I don't judge any mum for any way she chooses to mother. I tip my cap to the mums who breastfeed and I nod understandingly to the mums who don't. I'm not an expert and these are just my own personal experiences.

Before I had Pearl, I made the decision I would bottle feed. Those I mentioned it to told me not to feel guilty about making that choice, as though what I was telling them was a really dirty secret or I was breaking some kind of rule. I had moments when I questioned whether I should try it again but I was so fearful after what happened with Darcy and so acutely aware that my feeding experience with her had contributed to my plummeting mental health at that time that I stuck to my convictions and bought the bottles and steriliser.

It helped that because Pearl's birth was so smooth and calm, I was in a very different place physically, emotionally and mentally. I had a great experience to reflect on, a lot of support around me and was making choices I was confident with. Furthermore, Darcy was the perfect example of a healthy, happy child who did not appear to have suffered from being put on a bottle. Liam was on my side – he wanted all of us to be happy and he was thrilled that he could feed his baby too. Again, it was the right choice for us.

I think breastfeeding is truly amazing and every woman who does it for a day, week, month, year or more is incredible. Particularly those who overcome adversity, like my friend Clare, who could only feed from one breast. I salute their strength. But I don't look at those of us who haven't been able to do it and think we are weak. There is no comparison or judgement made. I know my limits and I know I couldn't have gone through that experience again. I breastfed Pearl on the day she was born and then that evening we took the bottles out and had the formula ready. She fed and slept well from then on – we were both happy and I bonded so quickly.

I didn't encounter any judgement from family and friends; they understood why I had made the decision and supported me. I was forthright in my social posts about my choice, sharing how confident and comfortable I was and was not looking for advice on the subject. I had a mixed response but I felt assured I was doing what was best for our family. If it helped at least one other mum out there be confident in sharing her choices (whichever they were), then even better.

It amazes me how many people feel it is their right to comment, positively or negatively, about women breastfeeding. Like the story I am about to share. Once upon a time, I was sitting in school reception, waiting for Darcy to finish an after-school club, and I was bottle feeding Pearl. To be truthful, I was feeling a little bit harassed, tired, hormonal and frankly AMAZED that I had managed to leave the house on time at all, and just glad to be sat sorting the feed (you know what it's like when you want to keep them in a routine!). One of the school dads came bounding in and then stopped short when he saw me. 'Oh, you are bottle feeding,' he said, surprised. 'I thought all the real mothers breastfed?' I kid you not, those were his exact words. I'm glad my friend was there as a witness because I'm sure if I repeated the story without her, people would think I'd made it up. The audacity of him!

I took a deep breath and let rip at him, both barrels. I was in no mood for this but even if I had been on top form, why would I have sat and taken it?! I said I was pretty sure I was a real mother since it wasn't that long ago I'd pushed this very real baby out of my very real vagina in my very real home (top tip, ladies: say 'vagina' with enough conviction and you're halfway there in an argument with a dim-witted man!).

He replied sheepishly, 'Sorry, but to be honest, I am glad you aren't, I wouldn't want to see you getting everything out in the school foyer.' WHAT?! It's very rare that I'm speechless but he stumped me. I couldn't believe it. Which way would he have preferred I feed MY baby? With a bottle or 'getting everything out in the school foyer'? Just a snapshot of the sort of thing we women have to deal with on a daily basis. Obviously, he's now crossed off my Christmas card list but I try to be extra nice to his wife since she has to live with such a buffoon, ha!

Here's another 'funny' story for you in a similar vein. Years ago, after I had joined the single parents club and was enjoying the freedom of a rare night out, I met up with a few friends, who brought along some of their friends. I instantly clicked with one of them – let's call him Richard to protect his identity. Do shorten that to whatever you like.

He had a daughter too from a previous relationship so I felt a shared understanding. The conversation and several bottles of wine flowed between us all, with interesting, non-confrontational discussions about the meaning of life. We fell onto the subject of breastfeeding. There was a general debate about which was best (some of the women in the group said they wanted to when they had children, some said they didn't) and suddenly Richard stepped in with an absolute beauty: 'It's bottle feeding or shit tits really, isn't it, ladies?!'

Maybe in his mind he was trying to support those women who didn't want to breastfeed. I am giving him the (massive) benefit of the doubt here, I know.

At the time though, rage bubbled up inside me. I erupted: 'DID YOU JUST SAY BOTTLE FEEDING OR SHIT TITS? ARE MY TITS SHIT, RICHARD?!' I said, a bit more loudly than I meant to. As I said it, I grabbed both my boobs and aggressively jiggled them at him (cheers for that, wine). He looked suitably chastened as I rattled on about how my breasts were for me and to feed a child but I certainly didn't think about men in that equation. I may have said something like, 'My tits are not there for your personal sexual pleasure, RICHARD.'

We both apologised – him for saying what he said and me for shouting at him. In fairness, he felt terrible the next day and contacted me to apologise again. I tried to explain how passionate I am about women's bodies and the choices we should be able to make without external pressure. My breasts may have only fed Darcy for a short time but my point still stood – although I probably shouldn't have yelled that point at him. I remember asking him if the mother of his little girl had breastfed and he said no, she had bottle fed. I wondered if that was her choice. Did she feel under pressure to look her best because the father of her child was worried her tits would be shit? I hope not.

Your body is LOVELY. I need to make this point because, unbelievably, in this day and age, women are still conditioned to believe we should give birth, breastfeed for at least a year and then, miraculously, have bodies that spring back into slim, taut shapes.

Often, we are forced into exercising too soon, dieting, thinking about the way we look, when we can have sex again and how 'bad' will our boobs be at a time when self-care should be the priority. Though if pushing yourself to return to your original weight is part of your self-care then I totally get that too, as long as it's your choice and not because you feel you 'should'.

When I fell pregnant for the first time, I carried my bump proudly. I put a bit of weight on but that was OK because, surely, that's normal. I may have eaten for two on occasion but nothing excessive or worrying. When I came home with Darcy, I still had a baby bump. It looked like I was still pregnant with a secret baby that had decided not to come out. The midwife told me not to worry because my tummy would 'just shrink back down again'. OK, I thought, great, one less thing to worry about.

Nine years later (and another baby) and I'm still waiting! How long can I call it post-baby weight before it is just a bit of regular fat?! Turns out, it takes a lot of work to get back to your pre-baby body and maybe we should focus on a new type of body post-baby. Our bodies have changed, so why shouldn't we celebrate that? Not give ourselves such a hard time to turn them back to 'perfect' when they've just done the most perfect thing they'll ever do – made new life!

I'm sometimes asked if I am pregnant, generally through my online community but occasionally an acquaintance will message me asking if I am about to make an 'announcement'. I try not to take offence. I'm a curvy lady so it would be easy to be a bit pregnant without people seeing, I talk a lot about being broody and I'm in an age bracket where people make babies. I get it.

But no, I'm not, and I don't think it's a question any woman should be asked. Wait for her to tell you if she is, otherwise just *shh* for goodness' sake. It is both an insulting (to many) and possibly dangerous question – you have no idea what her story is around weight or pregnancy or lack of pregnancy. You don't know if someone has been trying to conceive for a long time and you asking will cut them deeply, or perhaps someone has tragically just suffered a baby loss and having to tell you they're not pregnant would be horrendous. Unless a woman is literally looking like she's eaten a basketball for breakfast, don't say anything!

Sometimes 'concerned' people will want to know when I am going to hit the gym. I have never hit the gym, before or after babies. I am a natural plus-size girl and I am confident in my own skin. OK, there are things that have changed, I have stretchmarks and the tummy jibble that I mentioned earlier, but this body is still here, dancing on through its fourth decade after two gorgeous babies.

After I had Pearl, it was the only time that I have looked at myself and felt fat. I don't use that word lightly. I rarely feel negatively about my body but this time I couldn't squeeze back into all my lovely clothes. I could notice the difference moving around – it was harder and I didn't like it. So I made a concerted but not drastic effort to eat better, drop a few pounds (about 30 in total) and I now feel happy as I am. I won't be walking the runway anytime soon but this is my normal and I'm OK with it. I don't want to live a life hating how I look. I think one of the secrets to happiness is body acceptance and love. A bit like forgetting to put the rubbish out, the bin men go past and you think 'Oh no!', but then immediately just think, 'Meh, it's not the end of the world.' Hmm, totally just compared my body to a bin of rubbish. Oops!

## Mum Body Manifesto

1. Your body is amazing. It has grown and nurtured another human while keeping you alive in the process. Then it has given birth to that tiny being, in whatever way it has been able to. If you stop and properly think about it, it's an absolute, total miracle.

2. It is your body. It may not feel like it during pregnancy, labour, birth and nursing when your focus is all on your baby, but it is still your body. If a medical professional suggests or does something that you are not comfortable with, speak out. Your partner needs to respect this too.

3. Embrace your mum body. Whatever it turns out to be. If you are happy and healthy that is all that matters. Don't berate yourself for a jibbly belly – you made a baby, whoop!

4. Be who you are. If you know you won't be happy until you are back to your pre-baby weight then do something about it in a sensible manner. Just as I don't want to feel pressured to go to the gym, detox and diet, you may not want to feel bad if that is

exactly what you need to do. It's a girl code of allowing each of us to be who we are without judgement or ridicule.

5. Baby benefits. I am not good at pregnancy; I don't relish it for all sorts of reasons I have talked about in this book. However, parts of my body truly blossomed before and after giving birth, like my glowy-AF skin and the thickest, strongest hair you've ever felt in your life. My nails were also stronger and healthier and I felt all bright-eyed and bushy-tailed. Also, for a blissful while I had absolutely fantastic boobs – yassss. Sometimes you gotta take the perks where you can.

6. Health and happiness are key. Those are the things we should aspire to. Eating nutritious meals, factoring exercise into our daily routines (do what I say, not as I do here), finding a little time for ourselves and not sweating the small stuff. They are basic rules but can be so hard to stick to. Take a walk to the park or shops rather than driving. Make a healthy eating plan for the week and enjoy fresh fruit. You've got this!

7. *Pelvic floor alert. Whatever your views on exercise, your pelvic floor is one area not to ignore and it's the easiest exercise to do. Anytime, anywhere, a recommended 10–15 muscle squeezes will help. Don't involve your stomach or bum muscles, you need to isolate your pelvic floor. If you haven't done it before, try it now as you are reading this – it's important. In France, they give every new mother ten free physical therapy sessions to help strengthen her pelvic floor and teach her the skills to continue the practice. That's how seriously they take it and we should too. Are you squeezing as you read?*

8. *Booby trap. Bosoms change shape and sag with motherhood and age. I know friends who moan theirs are too big or too small, that if they could just have a little lift, a bit more or a bit less, then they would be happy. Girls, whatever your boobage, after breastfeeding, when your boobs have settled into what they will be post-children, buy a really lovely bra. Something that does a proper job but also makes you feel fantastic. It may be a bra of incredible sexiness, comfort, beautiful fabric or colour. Be proud of what you have.*

Ultimately, my lovely readers, the absolute honest truth of this entire chapter is that the topic bores me senseless. I know that sounds nuts when I have just given you a whole chapter on it but I felt I ought to say my bit and then put it to bed.

Why do we need to chat about women's bodies so much? Why are we still talking about it, commenting on them, pointing out flaws, praising the too thin and smugly assessing those who are different from the norm? Whatever 'normal' may be. Let's stop the debate, embrace acceptance, celebrate each other for who we are and carry on our lives in our own body beautiful way. Bodies are just fleshy sacks with meaty sticks pointing out the sides (your limbs, I mean, not the other fleshy, pointy stick . . .) I think I'd better stop typing now and move on.

# Chapter 11

## Things I Wish They Had Told Me: Pentland on Parenting Propaganda

Right, listen up, *mes petits bonbons* with a sprinkle of glitter on top, it's the stage in proceedings where I give you . . . horn tooting, drum rolling, jazz hands waving . . . The Mother of All Lists. You know I love a list, the more I have the happier I am, and I have shoehorned many into this book already. I have shared my innermost thoughts, talked about my difficult family history and given you full, unedited gory birth stories. Now it's time to collect all my motherhood wisdom, experience and wit together in one big showstopper (I'm really amping this up!).

Below are the things I wish I had been told or had known before embarking on this crazy roller coaster parenting ride. Buckle up, baby!

1. **Feel the fear and do it anyway.** American academic and writer Elizabeth Stone once said, 'Making the decision to have a child – it is momentous. It is to decide forever to have your heart go walking around outside your body.' This is the closest description to being a mother I can imagine. Then, when you have two children, your heart isn't shared, it is simply doubled. I'm assuming

this keeps going the more babies you have but so far I'm at two, so I'll keep you posted!

2. **When is the perfect time?** I am often asked this question. There isn't a perfect time, just use your best judgement and jump in. Things change and there are pros and cons in every situation but if you wait for perfect then you may well wait forever.

3. **Manage expectations.** I was so excited throughout my first pregnancy. I thought this was exactly what I had always wanted and dreamt of and now I was ready for it. It was going to be a great big life fix-all. Ridiculous, now I come to think of it – the sheer naivety and blind faith I had that all would be well – more than well, amazing! In truth, sleep-deprived, suffering from PTSD and emotional, I couldn't believe the reality was so different from what I expected. I had built myself up for the biggest fall and been taken in by the version of motherhood presented by a society who wants us all to keep procreating. The funniest thing of all is that I would (and did!) do it all again, so the dreamy adverts of perfect mums and celebs making it all look so easy may be propaganda, but it's addictive propaganda!

4. **Learning from the past.** As a parent, you look back on your own childhood with fresh eyes.

You realise how little your own parents actually knew and how much they were winging it, before 'winging it' was even a term used for child rearing. Some of us are luckier than others and carry little baggage from childhood, others have more than we can carry. All of us have been shaped by those experiences and have a responsibility to take the best bits forward and not repeat the worst. This is going to sound harsh, but one of the things I learnt from my upbringing was how I didn't want to parent like that in the future. Although I'd never wish my childhood on my worst enemy, I'm grateful I had it because it's made me who I am today and, at the risk of sounding like a total knob (again), I think I'm OK.

5. **Baby blues.** What a funny old name for it. It evokes images of a 1950s housewife drying a solitary tear on the edge of her apron and then carrying on with baking a delicious cherry cake. It feels almost romantic and dismissive at the same time. But what do you call it? There are so many levels and variations on mental health in motherhood. Whether you are struggling with hormones during pregnancy or diagnosed with post-natal depression, your issues are important. Do not allow others or yourself to dismiss these feelings – they are real, powerful and must not be ignored.

6. **Use your voice.** Speak up. I know this is easier said than done when you are weighed down by the dark cloud hovering overhead, the Emptiness surrounding you or the Dementors swirling. However you refer to it, if you are feeling sad, low, depressed, you don't need to label it, just talk about it. There are people who can navigate you through these times and I urge you to speak to them. It doesn't matter whether this is a moment, weeks, months or something you have dealt with throughout your life, it is valid and often there are things that can help. I have been there, most notably after giving birth to Darcy and during my pregnancy with Pearl. Both times it took me a while to open up and speak about it but as soon as I did, something shifted. It wasn't solved instantly but it was a start. I think we have a responsibility to those who are not yet mothers to make sure PND is openly discussed and treated as we would physical wounds.

7. **Be honest.** I used to believe that if I was honest about how low I was feeling someone would declare me an unfit mother and take my baby away. I know that sounds really extreme but when you're not firing on all cylinders, it's easy to catastrophise. I thought people would judge me and consider me weak. This didn't happen. In fact, I was helped and supported and felt very loved. If people judge you then they are not those

who you should be around. Asking for help is a sign of strength and you should never be scared to speak out.

8. **Instant bond.** LOL. I assumed there would be a 'great rush of love' for my baby (I'd heard this phrase time and time again) and that there was something wrong with me as a mother if I couldn't feel it. Every book told me I would look at my baby and fall in love. I looked at my baby and felt confusion. I knew I would lay down my life for this tiny thing and that was unconditional love, but I didn't have the rush of adoration everyone talks about. There was no overwhelming flood of warmth through my body. It happened gradually and this is another thing people don't talk about – you are not abnormal, a monster or unfit to be a mother. If you have been through a traumatic birth experience this can also affect how you feel about motherhood. Take your time and get to know your baby, the love will come.

9. **Good enough is good enough.** Just this. Be confident in the choices you make for your child and your family. It is good to seek advice if you feel you need it but pay attention to your instincts. We are all just muddling through but we also often know more than we think we do. Trust those decisions you make. If you can put

your hand on your heart and know you are trying your best then that's good enough.

10. **Fed is best.** I have covered this in my Bodies & Boobies chapter but I cannot leave it off this list. Breastfeeding is hard and nobody tells you quite how tough it can be. There are those who take to it instantly, others persevere and some stop. Any of these things are OK if they are right for you and your baby.

11. **You aren't alone.** Whether you are close to your mum, other family members or have a good network of great mummy friends, talk to them, let them help you when you need it. It took me a while to realise how much great female support surrounded me and even longer to open up to them about how I was feeling, but it has been a lifeline for me. I now have some brilliant mummy friends I can share the highs and lows with and I'm so thankful for them.

12. **Tell it like it is.** My friend Esther is so good at sharing the harder aspects of parenting. She does it with humour and honesty that makes you cry-laugh as you nod at how completely relatable whatever she's saying is. What she doesn't do is try and qualify it with some fluffy parenting disclaimer like '. . .but it's all worth it!' Guys, we all know it is worth it. Just because

we moan about our day does not mean we will then say, 'That's it, I'm sending the kids back to where they came from, I am done with this.' It goes without saying that we would die for our children. So there really is no need to caveat every complaint with a 'love them really' disclaimer – it's OK to have a little moan.

13. **Leave the house sometimes.** More specifically, embrace toddler groups. The law of averages states that there will be another parent there on your wavelength. There is bound to be at least one kindred spirit among the soft play balls. It is an ideal opportunity for your child to have fun away from the home environment, for you to join in the fun without being distracted by the laundry or phone, and you get to sit down with a coffee and an adult who doesn't want to talk about Peppa Pig all day. It's a win-win.

14. **Give yourself a focus for the day.** If the weather is bad and you are staying at home, make an event of it. Build a den of blankets and cushions or make a nest on the sofa, bake cakes together, bring the paints out and spend the afternoon snuggled up in front of a film. If the weather is good then head off to the park for an hour, or to the shops to pick up groceries, or pop into your local library. They don't have to be big achievements or chores, just something to punctuate the

very long hours ahead of you before the slide into bath- and bedtime. Sometimes my best days with the girls are the simplest. It's so much better to have a pyjama day and embrace it, rather than discover you are all still in your My Little Pony PJs at teatime, feeling hopeless and a tiny bit out of control. Own it, my friends!

15. **Make new friends.** God, I know this is chilling. I struggled with this for a long time. When Darcy started at school, I spent ages skirting around other mums, unsure how to infiltrate a group or start a conversation. Making the effort in the playground does pay off and other parents may be relieved that you are making the first move. It's a game of who is the least shy, I reckon. It took me months to settle into a network of school-gate mums even though they were all really nice. You don't have to be best buds but it's nice to have someone to stand with while you wait for the gate to open, discuss school concerns with or talk to about something completely unrelated to your little darlings! You never know, they might just become your best friends – #esterandlouiseforever!

16. **Find your media tribe.** When I was pregnant with Darcy, social media was in its infancy too. There weren't lots of mummy bloggers, vloggers or Instagram accounts. Now it is easy to

find like-minded mums on social media – as well as represented in factual and fictional books or cracking good TV like *Motherland*. These worlds show you how the secret things you may worry about around parenting are not just your fears, they are often shared. We are not alone and oh, the relief when you find out other people feel the same way you do!

This piece of advice does have its pitfalls, though. Don't follow anyone on social media who makes you feel bad or inadequate – you need to find the people who make you feel lovely. Furthermore, unless you have a strong constitution, don't hang around forums for too long. It can be a great space to ask a question but there are some who enjoy feeding on others' vulnerability. It can also lead you down a path of seeing things you can't unsee, like #penisbeaker – the conversation thread that nearly broke Mumsnet! It's a difficult place to navigate successfully. Ultimately, all the noise around parenting can be turned down instantly so don't be too distracted by it, just enjoy the best bits.

17. **Hire staff.** OK, I'm not talking *Downton Abbey* styley, although I would be the first one to put my hand up for a butler. What I am really saying here is if you can afford a little bit of help, go for it. Sometimes you can't do it all. Employing

a cleaner or paying someone to do the ironing could allow you more time with your children, less stress when you come home from work or that extra hour so you can go for a run (or in my case, a walk to the shops). As I have mentioned earlier in my Working Motherhood chapter, organising childcare and not feeling guilty is also important if that is what is needed. This bears repeating: Do Not Struggle Alone. If there is a way to make things easier then take it. I say this having been in both positions of being a working mum relying on nap times and evenings to get my job done and as a mum being able to afford a nanny. There are more creative ways to find help too – perhaps you could come to a reciprocal arrangement with another mum. Don't be a martyr if you don't have to.

18. **Reward yourself.** This is a virtual pat on the back at the end of the day. No biggie. No balloons, party poppers or cases of champagne. Just quiet acknowledgement that you made it through the day, whether it was a good or bad one, the children are in bed and now it is time for you. Have a bath, even if you don't need one! I know, the decadence of it. I find a hot bath, a few candles and a glass of wine (or mug of hot chocolate) is the quickest way to relax at the end of the day. Hey, putting on your heels and a slick of red lippy and going high

kicking out of the front door may be more your style, and who am I to judge?! I can head to a party or the sofa with the best of them, although these days the ratio of nights out to nights in is pretty stacked in one direction.

19. **Call me by my name.** When I was pregnant and just after giving birth, I was often spoken to in the third person – 'How is Mum feeling today? Has Mum fed Baby yet?' When Darcy started a specific club, her teacher (who knew me and would use my name outside of the club when I'd see her elsewhere) would say, 'Hello, Darcy's mum.' Which I always found odd, because I never said, 'Hello, Darcy's teacher.' I just used her actual name like people do in the real world. I am often called 'Darcy's mum' and 'Pearl's mum'. My name is Louise, thank you very much, and as well as being a mother of two glorious girls, I am also a Person in My Own Right. I wonder if my name will ever be used again or if I will be collecting my pension and signing 'Darcy & Pearl's mum' on the forms?!

20. **Banish guilt.** A pointless emotion. Stop it NOW. Don't entertain it for one moment and don't pass it on to your children. No good ever comes of feeling guilty so let that go immediately. You don't deserve it.

21. **Welcome back.** The loss of self is temporary. For the first few hazy, relentless years it is hard to separate the woman from the mother. Things do get easier and you will have yourself back so don't panic. Remember the old but true cliché that you will look back on the baby years and realise how quickly they went. When you are in the middle of them, you feel they will go on forever but, looking back, you will see what a short time in your life that was. You will also look back and only remember the best bits because your brain is clever like that. Careful, you might get pregnant again!

22. **Make lists.** Hahaha, this is a list and one of the points on the list is to make a list! Look, I know list-making is controversial. Some people swear by them, others swear at them. I am a totally listy person. I have been known to draw up a master list of lists to make. But I do know they can induce anxiety quicker than a toddler careering around the house with a permanent marker pen. Again, I say unto you, if the list system works for you do it and, if not, run free, child. Without pens though, yeah?

23. **Do what you can.** I can start the day with a long list of things to do and end the day with an even longer list. How does that happen?!

Things seem to migrate to it. Don't beat yourself up about all the things you haven't done. Did you put the washing on? Did you do a food shop or cook dinner? Did you laugh with your child? It's unlikely some of those things were on your list but just because they weren't doesn't mean you haven't achieved anything. It's about using the list as a help, not as a stick to beat yourself with. Things will get done.

24. **All the feelings.** Motherhood is an exhilarating roller coaster of emotions that you can never get off. You can feel invincible and overwhelmed, elated and depressed, lonely and suffocated, adoring and irritated, ALL IN ONE DAY. If you meet other mums who admit to this then do not let them go. They have the makings of best friends.

25. **Children are their own people.** Which is wonderful, thrilling, surprising and sometimes terrifying. As they start to talk and have their own thoughts and views, you encounter a whole different set of problems. I have included some of my favourite Darcy stories in this book, partly for your enjoyment and because if I write them here, I will never forget them. Like a few years ago, when I took Darcy to a nearby garden centre that also has a playzone.

We would often go straight after school and meet other mums and children there. Now, this play area should be paid for but as we turn up just before it closes, the children always pop in for a free ten-minute play while we order toasted sandwiches. One weekend, we went in for breakfast, a change to the usual routine. As I was paying for the food, I also asked to buy a ticket for the playzone because it wasn't ten minutes before closing and I knew she'd be in there a good while. Darcy looked at me, horrified, and said, 'But, Mummy, you don't normally pay, we just open the gate and go in for free!' The lady at the till raised her eyebrows while I turned a nice shade of crimson. That'll teach me!

26. **Count your blessings**. I think feeling grateful is my default #attitudeofgratitude. When things start to overwhelm me, I know I need just a little bit of time to gather my thoughts, acknowledge them, and list all of the positive things I have in my life.

27. **I wish I had known . . .** No, you don't really. If any one of us truly knew what we were letting ourselves in for, we may just not have done it. So, if you haven't yet had children, burn this list, and if you have, frame it.

# Chapter 12

# Hey, Mum Up There

I am often asked about how I cope with Mum's death, especially by those who have lost a parent themselves. The truth is, I was seven years old and too young to understand what dying meant. The initial pain turned into sadness and then numb acceptance. It is said that there are five stages of grief and, as an adult, they are very familiar to me: denial, anger, bargaining, depression, acceptance. As a child, I think I was stuck on the first for a long time. Now I can accept the situation and see bereavement as part of life – not obtrusive or detrimental but almost as a help. It reminds me to appreciate things and gives me a greater insight into how others might be feeling.

I accept that there is a mum-shaped hole in my life but this shifted when I had children. The pain associated with Mum now is around what she has missed – me growing up and giving her grandchildren. She isn't here to see them, play with them, be the brilliant granny I know she would have been. I fantasise about us having a brilliant relationship, her coming to my photoshoots and red carpet events, enjoying some of the benefits of my career. We would be super close and her support would be invaluable. However, I know that the reality may well have been different. I have a similar temperament to hers, headstrong and wild, we could have been thick as thieves or at loggerheads. I will never know and, in some way, it is a blessing that I don't because then I can maintain the perfect fantasy.

There is no doubt that she would have adored Darcy and Pearl, who both have Jane (her name) as their middle names. I talk to them about Granny a lot and Darcy knows she is in heaven. Mum would have been wonderful with them, spending time teaching them the crafts she was so interested in and so brilliant at. She would have loved coming to their school plays and sports days.

I think of the strong female thread in our family – my mum's mum, wonderful Granny Gill, and my mum, both gone and in heaven now, and then the three women here on earth – me, Darcy and Pearl – with my job to lead the pack till we all meet again, because I truly believe we will. It is a positive, comforting way to think about it and I rely on my spiritual beliefs.

I do still cry about Mum, sometimes something will trigger a memory and totally floor me. This is when humour really helps. My coping mechanism has most definitely been laughter. Digging deep into my dark humour and pulling out a dead mum joke is always a way to find the light in the darkness – even if you do sound a bit weird to those around you who aren't in the 'club' and don't 'get it'.

I had my darling mummy for 2,794 days. I know it may sound weird to count it out like this but calculations soothe me. It was my entire lifetime until I was seven but for her it was a heart-wrenching blink of an eye. When Darcy was 2,794 days old, I looked at her and marvelled over how small she was and how utterly devastating leaving her would be. A mother's job is to equip their child for the future, enable them to be the adult they want to be and support them as they achieve and fail. Mum had known she wasn't going to be able to do that. That must have been agony for her and it breaks my heart all over again to think about it from her perspective.

I have thought about all the things I would say to Mum if we had one more day together, or even just an hour. I have shared this online in the past but I am keen to repeat it here, with you. Partly because I want to ask you to do something for me. If you can, I want you to put this book down for a moment and call or message your mum, or a maternal figure you are close to. Tell them you love them or something that you know they would like to hear. Maybe thank them for who they are and what they have done for you. If there have been cross words or a rift, face it if you can. There is no time to lose because we have no idea how long any of us will be able to say things. Don't wait, the time may never come. I would love for you to do this for you and for my mum. Losing her has taught me the importance of cherishing the people I love and the everyday, no matter how mundane. That's an incredible legacy for her to have given me and I hope it encourages you too. Here are some other things I would say if she was sitting opposite me:

1. **'Mum, I am so, so happy.'** I really am and I want her to know that more than anything else. At the moment, my life is almost perfect. I have two amazing children, a wonderful fiancé, a happy home and an exciting career. It would only be better if she was still here. I want her to know that family rifts have healed and that Dad has turned his life around. That's because some years ago he met the fantastic Tina . . .

2. **'Mum, you would like Tina.'** I wish Mum could have met Tina. Which sounds strange because she is my dad's wife so has technically taken Mum's place. The thing is, Tina is wonderful. We struck lucky with her. My Aunty Judith

(Mum's sister and best friend) tells me often how much she likes Tina and I know Mum would approve too.

3. **'Mum, your death didn't scar me.'** It taught me so much and I really am OK. I worry about choices I have made and their effect on Darcy, like moving house, divorce and meeting somebody new. I am sure Mum was preoccupied with what her absence would mean for my life. It was traumatic for a long time, a brutal learning tool, but I really have come through it and taken the positives from the situation. Like cherishing every single day.

4. **'Mum, you have two gorgeous granddaughters.'** They have the most beautiful souls and they make me happy and proud every day. Since Mum's death, five girls have been born into our family and four of them have been given Mum's name, Jane, as their middle name. Mum, you are loved by so many and your name lives on.

5. **'Mum, I'm sorry I lose so many things.'** I know she would be frustrated by the amount of things I misplace. I can hear her now saying, 'For goodness' sake, Louise, look after your things.' Some lost items were treasures from her and my grandmother, things left to

me when they died. How could I have lost them?! I am hopeless with everything; in fact, I am most likely to be referred to as the girl who 'would lose her head if it wasn't screwed on'. I am going to make a big effort not to be so scatty, I promise.

6. **'Mum, I STILL don't like ham.'** Mum tried to encourage me to eat it so often. She had a best friend, Jill, who I have mentioned before with her hilarious nickname of Jilly-Willy-Botty-Bare-Bum. Jill's son Richard ate ham. Mum would continually say, 'But Richard likes ham,' and even at a very young age I would say, 'Just because Richard likes ham doesn't mean I do.' I still don't. It's vile.

7. **'Mum, I am sorry I don't visit your grave.'** I have never come to terms with her grave or the idea that she is buried in the ground. I find the cemetery a really creepy, scary place and I don't like being there. When I was little, I didn't want my dad to stand near me when we went (I just wanted to be alone with Mum) and so he'd sit in the car and watch me from afar. As an adult, I stopped going as much. I felt guilty about not wanting to visit for a long time, worried that showed a lack of respect. As an adult, I know that is not the way to remember her. I parent

my children the way she did with me and that is how I honour her. Every single day. Her ethos is alive in me and I hope it will be repeated if and when my girls become mothers.

8. **'Mum, I see you in every sunrise and sunset.'** She isn't in a grave, she is in so many sunrises and sunsets. This probably sounds unhinged but I actually feel her in the sky. Particularly those sunrises or sunsets that are lit with hues of orange, pink and red. She is in them, far away but looking directly at me. I was driving Darcy to school one day, she was only four, and there was an incredible winter sunrise. 'Look, Mummy,' she exclaimed, 'it's like Granny in heaven.' I hadn't told her how I felt about the sky and my mum. I just think Darcy felt it too.

9. **'Mum, you would love my life.'** She was a bit of an entrepreneur as I have already explained, and she loved crafting, sparkly things, glamour and fun. All the things that have weaved throughout my life and are now significant in my career. She would have wanted to know all about the parties, events and work issues I was dealing with. She could have travelled with me and shared my treasures, cosied up on my sofa and embraced my girls.

Having her in my life would have been magical and I'm forever grateful for the time we did have.

Two thousand seven hundred and ninety-four days of love from my mum that has lasted a lifetime.

# Chapter 13

# My Happy Ever After

Once upon a time, there was a little girl called Louise, with a wonky fringe and a doll tucked under her arm. She lived with her mummy and daddy and she was happy. Then her mummy died and she was very sad. Louise was sad for a long time. Then she wasn't. She met a prince and they married and had a bouncing baby girl but they didn't live happily ever after. So they divorced and stayed polite for the sake of their beautiful daughter.

Louise was sad for a bit and then she was happy again, just her and her girl. She did try and kiss a few frogs in the hope that one of them may be a real prince and then, one day, she struck lucky! A prince! Before she knew it, she found out she was going to have a baby and her family of two became a family of four and they all lived happily ever after. The end.

OK, my story is obviously very far from the end. I sincerely hope I have many, many years ahead of me but I also know, like fairytales, life changes. You go in directions you weren't expecting, which at times are dark and threatening and then just as quickly the sun comes out and joy returns. I have experienced enough of the darkness to know this, which is why when things are going well I want to celebrate, however temporary this state of happiness may be. I look at my family and it feels full and that is a lovely feeling to have. I really like where we are and how our unit of four operates, even though I never expected to have more than one child.

Everyone said it was so much easier going from one to two children. Apparently, the baby would just slot right into normal life – in fact, when you had a child already, you would barely notice the other one was there. The older one would entertain the younger one. There's nothing to it. Just another fish finger in the pan. Blah blah blah. Yet again, more parenting propaganda designed to lull you into a false sense of security.

Having another child was not easier. A newborn baby doesn't slot into the school run, after-school clubs, swimming and play dates. It doesn't sit quietly while you read to your other child. I had forgotten how much stuff I had to cart about too, the regular feeds and naps that needed to be factored in and the random crying for no reason (not me second time around, just the baby).

What is true is how quickly that phase passes. Before you know it, your baby is a toddler and you are suddenly hit by the odd bout of broodiness. My two girls are my world. Pearl is with me all the time and Darcy is at home for half the week and with her father for the other half. I am happiest when I have both under the same roof, playing in the house, running around the garden or safely tucked up in bed.

When Darcy is away, I have baby time with Pearl and we do the things that Darcy is too old for, like baby ballet, soft play and hanging out with other little ones. When Darcy is home, I focus on her more and she stays up later than Pearl so she and I have time together. Every year, I book a little trip just for me and Darcy and I hope this continues for as long as she wants to go away with me. I am hoping she still will as a teenager but that will probably be because I'm paying! Liam sometimes takes Pearl so Darcy and I can do something fun or she will join me for a work event if it is appropriate. She is so easy to bring to things, really polite and happy to go with the flow. When Pearl is a little bit older, I hope to have special one-on-one trips and adventures with her too. For now, though, we're enjoying our cute 'Mummy and me' days at the park or with toddler friends.

Darcy loved Pearl instantly but she soon realised babies can be a little tedious and won't come upstairs to play with her or behave like her dolls do. She was tenderly ambivalent. 'I love her,' she would say to me earnestly, 'but she *is* quite boring.' 'I feel the same,' I would respond, 'but all babies are the same. Very soon she'll start being super fun, I promise!'

Now Pearl is a toddler, she and Darcy often play together but Darcy has a list of things that Pearl is not allowed to touch. Darcy likes to play on her own terms and Pearl does not give a single shit about anybody's terms. A list of rules, drawn up and repeated by Darcy, means nothing to her. Like the L.O.L. Dolls rule: Darcy is clear that Pearl is not allowed, under any condition, to touch the L.O.L. Dolls, but Pearl wanders into Darcy's bedroom and, oh look, the L.O.L. Dolls are calling to me.

Darcy often hides toys in random places to stop Pearl finding them. This morning I found a Sylvanian family huddled behind the shampoo bottle in the shower. When Darcy is away, we keep her bedroom door closed. We respect her space as she is not always there to protect it herself and I know she feels the lack of control. Her bedroom is her sanctuary, so it is off limits to Pearl and her little friends with their curious tiny toddler fingers.

As the girls grow older, we can be more adventurous with our holidays, but right now our trips are chosen based on what works for young children. We learnt early on that a romantic minibreak to Nice with a four-month-old was neither romantic nor a break. Since then, we've stuck to UK-based day trips and Florida, because Disney is my happy place. I am not sure I can impress on you HOW MUCH I LOVE IT. Except to use capitals like I am shouting it at you. I love it so much Liam even proposed to me there, knowing it is the BEST place on earth to me! It is one of the few places in the world where I can switch off and forget all the hard things, not just the tough personal trials but the bigger global events.

I have already shared the story about the first time I went with my parents, when my mum knew she had terminal cancer but I didn't. She triggered a lifelong love of Disney and I feel so close to her whenever we go there. There is a ride called A Small World, which I remember being her favourite. We often talk with the girls about Granny in heaven wherever we are, but when we go back to Disney, we always head for this particular ride. It is 11 minutes long (yep, I timed it) and once, as the girls love it so much, we went on it six times (that's why I timed it, ha!). Totally magical and it always makes me smile, thinking of Mum.

Stepping out of my routine and taking a break from normality is so lovely. As a family, we reconnect when we are away from the house, chores and the general humdrum of life, and are more able to focus on each other. Holidays do still require routine when you are away with little ones but it is totally worth it.

Let's face it, you haven't experienced a family holiday until you have all shared a room together and a child has covered the carpet with salmon vomit two days into a ten-day trip. We laugh about it now but, my goodness, Fish Sick Week was a corker. I'd also like to add that there is no worse parenting moment than being in a holiday park swimming cubicle with wet, hungry children and having to dress everyone back into knitwear and denim. If you can complete that with only 30 per cent of you crying it was worth it. Again, I talk from experience.

Losing Mum when she was so young has been an ongoing lesson to me to grab every moment, cherish the time we have, use it wisely and spend it with the people we love. I know she would have loved our little family and I am proud of what we have created without her, a living memorial in a way.

I have parented alone. When my marriage ended, I gave myself a big talking-to. I knew I could do the single mum thing, batten down the hatches, devote my life to Darcy and work. Then Liam came along and I made it very clear that I was not looking for a father replacement for Darcy. I wanted someone who would understand I was a mother before anything else and be a friend to Darcy. Now I am one half of a parenting team and I think we make a pretty good job of it.

Liam is an incredible father to Pearl and takes a lovely paternal position in Darcy's life. We have very aligned ideas on how to parent and it is a relief and a joy to be able to share the everyday and the big decisions. There have been moments when I have made the final call on something Darcy-related because she is my child but I respect Liam's view and I listen to him. It will be interesting to see how we adapt as the girls get older.

We may be too young to remember *The Brady Bunch* but the American TV sitcom about the blending of two families was a big hit in the early 1970s. It told the story of a widowed father with three boys who marries a single mother with three girls and they all live in a lovely big suburban LA home with a housekeeper. It was a jolly, feel-good depiction of what was still seen as an unconventional set-up. It may have only run for five series but the term 'The Brady Bunch' is still used to describe stepfamilies. It makes you think of a warm, funny bonding of a big family. Which can be misleading because we all know real life is very far from Hollywood's depiction. Joining families and crossing over into others is a huge challenge. I think this is often underestimated.

I have been a stepdaughter a couple of times and I have a half-sister who I love dearly. I have been a step-sibling, first to two boys who came and then left our lives after nine years, and then again to Tina's children, Holly and Ben, who continue to be a close and important part of our family. In fact, Tina is the real heroine of this story, as she cracked the code for great step-parenting and encouraging strong bonds. As an adult, I have created my own blended family with Liam as a step-parent to Darcy. She benefits from having him and I'm so glad he's in her life. All these relationships are happy, safe and beloved. So here are my top ten tips for successful family blending, speaking as one who knows the perils and the triumphs . . .

### *Stepfamily Love*

1. *Don't rush. You and your new partner may fall in love quickly but that doesn't mean everyone else will find it as easy. You can't force this sort of relationship, whether it's between adult or child. I have been the child in this scenario and it was frightening and hard to deal with. Don't bandy the word 'family' about. Or talk about loving each other before everyone is ready. Take baby steps. When Liam and I were first together and he was spending time with Darcy, I would refer to us as a team. For Darcy, her family was me and her dad, not this new man who*

she liked but didn't know very well. It took us two years to call ourselves a family and that came with Pearl's arrival.

2. Don't try and buy a child's love. Children can see through this tactic. I did when I was a child and I was hugely mistrustful of what it meant. It is often covering up for something that is lacking. Children want time spent on them – this is so much more important than gifts. Liam didn't buy Darcy things but he did give her his time and attention. Their friendship built gradually and is all the stronger for it.

3. Set time limits. If you are encouraging a stepfamily to spend time together then manage expectations. Give everyone a clear structure of a walk or a lunch without trying to pull off an entire day together. This can cause stress, resentment and result in the time you are together being unenjoyable. Focus on short periods of time with a reason to gather. Little and often is so much better than long and unending. I think that is actually good advice for any family, particularly when you have teens to consider.

4. If you are the adult, be an adult. Set the example early on. However badly your stepchild may behave

*and however old they are, remember you are older and behave appropriately. I know I wasn't a very nice stepdaughter to Tina at first, after a chequered family history, but Tina was such a grown-up about the whole thing; she carried on being kind and loving and completely won me over. I have so much respect for her efforts.*

5. *Hold your tongue. In other, clearer words, don't slag anyone else off. However tempting this is, do* **not** *do it in front of the children or involve them in the conversation. This happened to me as a child. Somebody was incredibly rude about my family and it made me dislike that person instantly. I'm not saying 'don't ever have a good vent', but choose your audience and don't let that audience be the children.*

6. *Listen to your child if they raise alarms. I know this can be difficult as children may not like a new step-parent or situation and react negatively but, whatever they say, listen to them and use your parental instinct. Talk to the person involved and don't feel embarrassed about investigating something that turns out to be nothing. I wasn't listened to as a child so now I'm hyper aware. Not just with my own children but with other people's. Sometimes a child can't talk*

within the family unit but will trust an extended family member or friend. Keep listening.

7. Have healthy alone time together. Whether this is you and your partner planning a regular date night, or whether this is with your child away from the stepfamily set-up. It could be any combination but it doesn't have to involve all of you, all the time. Keep the bonds going.

8. Where possible, plan excursions. An activity that everyone can focus on, something enjoyable away from the home, really helps. It can distract from the tensions that build in the house and encourages step-parents and step-siblings to have fun together.

9. Treat all children equally. For a family to blend successfully every member must feel valued. There should be no favouring of your own children over someone else's. Tina did this so well and made me and my half-sister feel so loved and welcome. It stops resentment between children and helps a healthy relationship form. Try some house rules that focus on equality and fairness. (I know this one is REALLY hard.)

10. *Accept the past. If you are a step-parent it can be hard to hear children talking about memories that you weren't part of. This doesn't mean they are trying to wipe you out of their lives. They must be able to cherish the past as they move confidently into the future. Liam has no issue hearing Darcy reminisce, nor do we discourage her talking about the time she spends with her dad. There are no rules about what she can and can't talk about and Liam would never be upset or take it personally.*

I would be lying if I said I never struggle with motherhood now. I defy anyone to say they don't at times. I'm fairly selfish by nature and I need my own space. Children are little time suckers – they demand your attention and there's nowhere to hide. (Although occasionally the loo or utility room is quite a good place, except that is now the first place mine tend to look for me.) There is no let up, no annual leave (though, remember, if I get elected PM, I'll sort that out) and no sabbatical from mothering. You can't put your maternal head to one side and put on your free-and-single head instead. Once you are a mother you shoulder the responsibility that comes with it forever, but that's also the very best bit about it! You are always a mum, no matter how old they are or how far apart, they're forever your baby.

I love the feeling of having my hands and heart full all the time, of having an incredible bond with two people which is unique to us, our little girl gang. Being part of a community with other mums is a privilege and watching my children build their own friendships gives me such warm heart fuzzies. It feels like a selfish and selfless love at the same time.

I remember so clearly when I went to collect Darcy from her first day at school – she was sitting at her desk with her bag in front of her, patiently waiting for me, blonde curly hair all over the place and paint down her pinafore as a sign of a good day. I stood there in the classroom and I cried. My little Darcy, so small and yet already so grown-up and experiencing a world I am not a part of. The emotions of motherhood are many and plenty.

When I was little and life was tough, I would always look at other families and feel jealous. I wanted what they had – a loving family unit with two parents and a safe home to go back to. I now have the thing I coveted and I am just so unbelievably happy about it. There is an element of luck to how things have worked out so far, but I also like to think I helped make it happen. Working hard at my business and having great friendships have been partly responsible for my freedom. I have not had to stay in a relationship or situation for economic or social reasons, nor will I allow myself to be controlled after a childhood of it. I know I'm a good mummy, just like my mother was to me. I wish I could be more modest about it but there it is, ha! I think it would be very fair to say I'm absolutely living my very own happy ending these days.

*My Darling Darcy,*

I've written this letter a few times now and I'm struggling. You are so important to me that writing this letter feels like such a huge task. There is so much I want to say to you. I'll apologise now if this letter is wibbly wobbly higgledy-piggledy. I've decided it's best just to let it all out as I think it, because every time I try and order my thoughts I lose them.

I think the first thing I want to say is how much I love you. You are so special because you gave me my mummy heart. You taught me what it was to love another with all your soul and you showed me what real love is. When I think about how much I love you, I don't care how hard your birth was. I'd do it a thousand times over if it meant I had you every day of my life. When I talk about your birth, a little part of me worries that you will feel bad or guilty for it – please don't. You are worth every single second of it and more. I share the story because our experience can help other people and that's just *another* blessing of having you!

You were a planned baby. My whole life I'd wanted to be a mummy and God gave me you, so I say thank you a lot. When you were about three you asked how I had you and I said, 'You were a gift from God.' You smiled, thought about it for a while and said, 'What sort of paper was I wrapped in?' I always laugh about that.

I've made a list of some more of the funny little things you've said over the years. My all-time favourite is when you were about two and saw a mole that I have on my arm. You touched it and said, 'Oh, what's that?' I said, 'It's a little mole.' You replied, 'Uh oh! He should live outside!' Haha!

You bring such a warm energy to a room, delighting people you talk to with your good manners and charming humour. I hope that stays with you into adulthood because it's a bit of a winning formula! I love that you always strive to do the right thing and, generally speaking (unless it's sharing L.O.L. Dolls with your little sister), you have a generous spirit. You're a good person. I'm proud of you.

We've had a lot of funny moments, haven't we? I hope this list of some of my favourites makes you smile one day.

1. Mile-high sundae! When it was just 'the Mummy and Darcy Team', I decided we should go and visit our friends Marie,

Ryan, Scarlet and Luca (Sadie hadn't been born by then) in Seattle. I'd been feeling very down (you used to call it 'the sad time') and so I used my air miles to book us into first-class seats and travel in luxury! You were four and were being very well behaved on the flight. I was emotionally exhausted after a particularly difficult couple of months and told you I was going to have a little sleep. I said, 'If you need anything, just wake me up,' and you promised you'd sit nicely and watch your film.

Well, while I was asleep it turned out that you really, reeeaally knew how to travel in luxury! You wrote the flight attendant a sweet note and she was utterly enamoured by you. When I woke up, you were sat with your table out and a beautiful ice cream sundae, complete with cherry on top, ready to eat in front of you. Spoon in hand, you had the biggest grin on your face I've ever seen! Since then, you've managed to woo flight attendants into so many treats it's unbelievable – you've had Turkish delights, a platter of fresh strawberries, more pretzel bags than I can count and a badge from the captain! You certainly know how to jet set!

2. Disney adventures! This isn't really one thing but lots all rolled into one. I have loved with all my heart our many adventures to Disney World, our happy place! We love everything about it, don't we? Planning our trip, exploring the parks, matching our outfits, wandering round the resorts and, of course, the snacks! Soon, Pearlie will be old enough to join our Disney Girl Gang and we can go on the girls' trip we talk about so often!

3. Naughty cake! Another restaurant tale. Do you remember when I was super heavily pregnant with Pearl and we all decided to go out for dinner? We went to Pizza Express (one of our favourites) and they had a limited edition cake called the 'Sticky Toffee Bunt Cake'. It was nearly three years ago now you STILL tell everyone about the time when, as a joke, I called it 'Stick It Up Your Bum Cake'. I thought it would be a funny thing for five minutes but I think that's going to stay with us forever and ever now.

4. Hotel nights! You and I are both lovers of a good hotel night. You were only a

couple of weeks old the first night you stayed in a hotel with me (I have a photo somewhere!), when we travelled up to Manchester for a family party on your dad's side. Since then, we've stayed in hotels all over the UK, visiting family, we've tried out six Disney resorts, had a sea view apartment in Gran Canaria and even stayed in a hotel in Malaga with a giant slide in the lobby! I think my best hotel night with you, though, was on my book tour in 2019 in Leeds. We stayed in a Premier Inn (we both love that chain because it's always clean and always reliable) and I ordered us giant cheesey pizzas to eat in bed while we watched Disney videos on my laptop! We have fabulous fun, don't we?

You are a joy to be around. You love to dance to songs on the Alexa and you love to keep your bedroom super tidy. You don't enjoy school work too much (don't worry, nor did I) but you do like playing with your friends and making up games. You like cuddles and are really tactile. Sometimes, because I'm not naturally very huggy, you tell me I haven't cuddled you enough and we have some big squishes. I'm glad you remind me – I always want to give you big snuggles, I just forget because I'm wired differently to you.

My biggest goal for you in life is to be happy, healthy and safe. I'm teaching you your emotional worth and hopefully, Liam shows you how a man should treat a woman when you see how good he is to me. I'm working really hard now to give you some financial security because I want you to have the best life possible. I'm constantly saving money for you but I also want you to know the value of hard work. Always work smart and always do it with a glad heart. Don't treat anyone badly; the right choice might not always be the easy one but sleeping well at night is crucial and, eventually, you'll see it was the best option. Take the high road whenever you can and always go the extra mile. Celebrate your successes well but celebrate other people's more. All ships rise in high tides.

People are important. You are a people person, you enjoy having friends over and spend lots of time writing them sweet letters or drawing them pictures. Nurture your friendships because when the chips are down, they'll be there for you.

Look after your sister. She will need your calming energy to cool her hot head and you'll need her boundless enthusiasm when you need some motivation. You're perfect for each other; you were meant to be each other's sister. Take good care of her, protect her, respect her and love her.

Love easily. Don't let your heart grow scars from bad experiences, let love in and let yourself enjoy it. You are worth it. I don't mind if you find your life partner at 16 or 60. I don't mind if they're a man or a woman. I want you to respect yourself, love well and be happy. I can't guarantee I won't totally embarrass you when you bring the first one home but I promise you I won't do the Mummy Dance in front of them straight away!

I'm sorry for all the things I've gotten wrong already or all the things I might do wrong in the future. I'm sorry I didn't make it work with your dad and I'm sorry you had to grow up in two homes – I know that has been hard for you. I want you to know I didn't leave lightly, I thought (and still do think) it was for the best, but I know it hurt and that it doesn't make the endless to-ing and fro-ing any easier for you. Thank you for living that life to the best of your abilities. I hope you are able to take the positives from it all and that the negatives don't overshadow them.

I'm sorry I'm not better at maths to help you with your homework and I'm sorry I never go down the water slides on holiday with you because of my contact lenses. I'm sorry for all the times you want my attention and I'm working on my phone or laptop; I hope it will have been worth it in the end.

I hope when you're grown-up, we are still the best of friends. The other day you gave me a card and called me your 'best grown-up BFF'. Same to you, kiddo. You're my best nine-year-old BFF and long may that continue!

When you're older I want to do all the things I never did with my mum, your dear granny in heaven. I want to take you on shopping trips to London, visit spas, bargain hunt in charity shops and have cinema nights. I want to help you decorate your first home, watch you throw your first party and hopefully, one day, if you want them and can have them, hold your hand as you bring your own babies into the world. This bit of the letter has actually made me cry. The thought of loving your babies as much as I love you and your sister is a lot.

You've just come in from your walk as I type this. We're in a lockdown at the moment because of a big virus (Covid-19) and you've been out with Liam and your sister so I could write this letter. You said, 'Have you been sat there the whole time?' Ha! I could sit here and write to future you forever but I think I'll wrap this up, my sweet Darcy Bluebird, so I can come and be right there in the moment with you.

I'm proud of you, Darcy Jane. You are my first greatest achievement, you are completely and utterly wonderful.

**Be good, love you forever,**

**Mummy xxxx**

Dear Pearl,

My sweet Pearlie girl, I'm so excited to write this letter for you. I was nervous to write your sister's in case I got it wrong somehow, but now I've worked out what I'm doing, I feel relaxed and confident. I think that's a bit of a theme of our relationship, actually. You are my second precious baby and my second wonderful gift but you are certainly not second place. You are my second greatest achievement and I feel so lucky to have you and to have not one but TWO beautiful girls. Wow!

When I was pregnant with you, I worried that I wouldn't love you as much as your sister. I feel a bit guilty for writing that down in black and white but it's true. A mother's love for a child is so fierce that it fills your whole heart and mine was so full of Darcy that I didn't know how I would make space for you. Well, I shared my fears on Instagram (I wonder if that will still be a thing by the time you're old enough to read this?) and the other mums said: your heart doesn't halve, it doubles. Guess what? They were right! When you were born, my heart doubled in size and you filled every new space possible. I don't love you half, I love you whole. You are just as much my whole world as your big sister is.

At the time I am writing this you are only two but we've already had quite a journey! I'm sure you won't mind me admitting that you were a bit of a life surprise. The best kind of surprise but still, I wasn't expecting you! I had Darcy in my twenties and, after a traumatic birth and difficult introduction to motherhood, I didn't think I'd do it again. I was afraid of birth, afraid for my mental health afterwards and, overall, I felt a little bit broken.

Well, my gorgeous girl, in my thirties you arrived and you fixed it all! You are my healing child. You forced me to face my fears, overcome them and feel empowered. What a gift to give a mother, all on your very first day of life!

Did you know you have an amazing birth story? You were born at home in the kitchen-diner. I scooped you out of the birthing pool and held you on my chest, the first person in the world to feel you and kiss you. You were so soft and so content, just being curled up in my arms. Once your daddy and the two amazing midwives, Paula and Jane, had helped me out of the pool, I spent the entire day cuddling you! We sat on the sofa from

11am to midnight, wrapped up together in blankets, skin on skin, all snuggly warm, and it was beautiful. I cherish any still moments we have now because you have grown into a very, very bouncy ball of energy!

You love playing outside, climbing, bouncing, running and being on bikes, trikes and scooters. You love swings, slides, roundabouts and soft play centres. You love swimming with Daddy and running round the kitchen with your cousin Dexter. You love to copy everything Darcy does and you think she's so funny. You are fearless and enthusiastic and I'm excited to see how that develops as you grow. I love your zest for life – we should all be a bit more 'Pearl'!

I hope I am able to give you a stable life. I feel guilty that you only see your sister for half the week because she visits her daddy. I'll work my bum off every other way I can to provide a good, positive life for you because that's what you deserve. I hope you see the effort your daddy and I put into our relationship and that you are able to do the same too one day. As with your sister, I don't mind who you fall for or when (maybe even if) you do it; as long as you are loved, respected and cherished, I'm happy. Your dad though, I'm not sure he'll be letting you have girlfriends or boyfriends for a while – to him, you'll always be his baby.

*Pause the letter, you've just come in to pinch some of my chocolate buttons and dump a load of toys onto my lap. This is very standard behaviour, haha!*

You've only been here a short while so far but we've had some fun already. I love making lists so here we go:

1. Nice. This was your first proper holiday and you were four months old. Daddy and I wanted a little minibreak and we thought it would be no trouble to take you too . . . We were wrong but it was still lovely! My favourite memory was sitting by the pool, my feet in the water, holding you and feeding you a bottle of milk. You were so content, the water felt so lovely, it was blissful.

2. Christmas in the bushes! It was Christmas Eve and your daddy, sister, you and I had gone to the supermarket to do a massive food shop. We were having the whole family round and we wanted to cook up a feast for them. We arrived home, parked on the drive and began unloading all the shopping. I wanted to be as efficient as

possible so I took you (strapped in your car seat) out and looped the handle on my arm and in the other arm I carried three bags at once. Big mistake. I tripped up the step and fell! I knew I had you in my arms so I made myself fall in a way that I took the brunt (I couldn't walk on my foot for a week!) but you rolled off into the bushes! I looked up and you were lopsided (still in your seat, which was at a 90-degree angle) and smiling at me from the bushes, as though you'd just had a great little time!

3. Soft play. If there's one place in the world you love, it's soft play! We've spent many happy mornings plodding round the little playhouses, whizzing up and down slides (you have no fear and go down even the huge bumpy one at about 1,000mph!) and watching the other children. Sometimes you make little friends, sometimes you enjoy being in your own world. I love watching you enjoy yourself there. We're currently in a lockdown (we're on week seven right now) but when this is all over, I can't wait to be back.

4. Artie. Our next door neighbours have a dog called Artie and oh my goodness, do

you love him! You particularly like it when he makes his happy squeaky noise and you often talk about him when he's not outside playing with you. I love seeing you be so caring and joyful for another creature. Maybe you'll have a great affinity with animals when you grow up!

5. Your 'wheres'. Your favourite thing in all the world (after us, of course!) is your Where. Your Where is actually an old muslin cloth that we used to swaddle you in as a baby and, over time, it's become your comfort blanket. We think you started calling it the Where because we were always saying, 'Where's the blanket?' and you picked up on the wrong word but we think it's adorable and now it's stuck. I will, in time, wean you off things like the dummy but the Where can stay. Shall I let you in on a secret? Mummy is 35 and she has a little comfort cloth too. It's called Pillie and it lives under my pillow, ready to offer comfort whenever I want it. We're not so different, you and I.

I am loving every stage of you. I'm not feeling sad that you're no longer teeny tiny because your sister has taught me that every stage has amazing things in it. I'm grateful for my struggles the first time round because now I can be so much more relaxed with you. I don't fret over small things, I don't worry as much about you (even though you're such a little daredevil, hurtling up and down the stairs or running round outside with no fear at all!), we just enjoy it all.

What do I want for you when you're an adult? Joy. Happiness. Health. I want you to run at life with the same vigour as you tackle things now. I want you to feel valued and important. I want you to know you are absolutely adored by us all and I hope you will love us back just as much.

You are so young at the moment so it's hard to tell too much about you but I am loving getting to know you. Each day we spend together I feel like we learn a little more and, as the weeks go by, you are starting to play more and more with your sister, which is so lovely for my mummy heart to watch. I hope you grow into close friends and you have so many adventures together! I want you to love your sister and listen to her. I want you to take care of her (I've told her the same) but not to live in each other's shadow. You are both beautifully individual and there is space for each of you to shine.

As well as all the things I want you to do with your sister, or I want for us to do as a family, I'm also really looking forward to spending some one-on-one time with you. I'd love to take you on a special Mummy-and-Pearlie trip when you're a little bit older and I'd love to take you to work with me in London a few times before you start school. I hope when you're older we find things we can both do together and cherish forever.

Pearl Jane Pentland, you are pure joy! You came into my life by surprise, you healed a huge hole in my heart, you have been a ball of boundless fun and laughter and I can't wait to spend the rest of my life enjoying you! Once you grow and start showing more of your lovely little personality off, I might write you another letter with more life advice but for now, you're aceing it, my girl!

I love you more than I could ever write in a letter. You are total and utter joy, smiles and rainbows, biscuits and Peppa.

**Lots and lots of love forever and always,**
**Mummy xxxx**

Dear Darcy and Pearl,

A letter to both of you! Well, first of all, I hope we can all agree that you two and I are the best girl gang in the entire world! Nobody does bedtime duvet and videos like us, nobody does Nutella pancake mornings like us, nobody does co-ordinating outfits at Disney like us! OK, they might do, but we're happy, aren't we?

Thank you both for being brilliant. I'm so grateful to have you in my life. Not only have you healed my heart in more ways than you can imagine, you've also expanded it too! My heart and hands are very full!

So, here's the deal. You guys have to love each other forever and take care of each other. That's a big commitment but it's well worth it. There will be times when you might feel cross at each other or you might not want to be friends, but at the heart of you, you are sisters and you are special to each other. One day, hopefully in the far-off future, I will rest easy up with Granny Jane, knowing you will take care of one another.

Have patience with each other, accept you will have different interests, different loves and go with it anyway. Find your common ground and work on that. Maybe it will be Disney, maybe it will be something that isn't even invented yet! That's an exciting thought, isn't it?

If you have them, treasure each other's children. You will be aunties and those are special. Cheer for each other's successes and be available to lean on in times of failure. Laugh together, cry together, sing with wild abandon in the car together; you are flowers from the same garden and you were given to me to be sisters together.

I love you both equally. I know this will be a thing! Darcy, you're nine and have already started measuring and making sure things will be equal, like when you go through my jewellery or bags and ask who will have what when I'm finished with it. Smart and savvy, I like it!

You are both unique and I love the qualities you both have. So, I love you equally but I love different things about you and that's OK. You both have my whole heart.

I hope I always have a place in your hearts too and when you read this book, you will know and understand more about my journey to reach both of you. It hasn't always been easy but it's always been worth it, every bit a step closer to you.

**Love and cuddles to both of you forever and ever,**
**Mummy xxxx**

# Bonus Content: My Top 10 No-Guilt Motherhood Hacks

1. **Lists!** I love lists! I'm going to start this list by once more admitting my love of lists and telling you how much they help me. I've always loved a handy list of things I need to do during the day/week/month, but they can so often become a way of reprimanding ourselves for not getting everything done. Think of a list as a guide only. Tackle it how suits you best – split it up by how time-consuming a task is, or themes (like work, house, garden, children etc.). A list is not a binding contract, you do not need to judge yourself if yours flows on and on and nothing seems to get crossed off. You are busy living – looking after yourself AND children.

2. **The Pearl outlook.** MumLife doesn't come easily to me and sometimes I find it really flipping hard but spending so much time with Darcy and Pearl over the lockdown period has been a gift. What I have been able to notice so much is their

optimism. Even on the hard days, when things get tough, you can rely on your children to remind you of the bright side of things.

3. **Low-cost activities.** One of my favourite ever things to do with Darcy and Pearl, which doesn't cost a lot but can keep them occupied for hours, is making potions! We collect petals, flowers, glitter and get going. I am always on the lookout for new pretty little vases or bottles in charity shops, I give them a clean, and then they get a second use. You can find tons second hand online too if you're unable to get out of the house much. This can be customised to suit you – you can use jam jars and nature from the garden instead. Always supervise young children with glass bottles/glitter/small bits, of course.

4. **The Power of the Fort.** Inside, outside, it doesn't matter – a child will always go crazy over a fort! Grab as many sheets, duvets, cushions and pillows as possible and create a cosy corner inside for them to play in. Fill with toys and *fingers crossed* they should love it for hours. If you have the space, move outside, weather permitting – drag some chairs out and create a space on the grass for playing.

5. **Disney.** Yes, I'm including this here, it is my list and I shall Disney if I want to. Honestly, the time I have been able to reclaim as my own by putting a great classic Disney film on runs into the hundreds. I personally vouch for *Mulan* and *Tangled* as the perfect duo for an afternoon of peace.

6. **A Room of One's Own.** I'm lucky enough to be able to have separate rooms for Darcy and Pearl. They are mostly brilliant at sharing, but often want their own space – especially Darcy, who is growing up and finding her feet in her own shoes, developing her personality. I make sure the two of them know they can always have alone time, that they don't need to constantly be each other's source of fun.

7. **Tidy together.** Clean house, clean mind! You no doubt have toys in your work space and notepads in the cupboard, but you can make a game out of putting everything away. The more everyone puts in the right place, the more treats to enjoy later.

8. **Small goals.** Set small, specific goals for yourself and your family. It can be something as simple as 'today we will make a cake', but following

through on it brings a sense of achievement and hopefully, you get to eat some cake! Notice I didn't write 'today we will make a cake with no arguments and no mess and everyone will be happy' because this is real life. It is messy, and there are arguments. Just try to remember number 2 and The Pearl Outlook.

9. **A chat to end the day.** At the end of each day, talk with your kids about something you're looking forward to doing tomorrow, or something you liked about today.

10. **Look after yourself.** Yes, sounds simple enough, doesn't it? But it's not always so easy. In whatever time you have – whether it's five minutes before you really need to go to sleep, or a half hour at lunch, pause. Take stock of yourself, what you are feeling, and what you need personally. You are doing the best you can. And if you need help, reach out – online, to friends, to supportive family. Good eggs will be there for you.

# Acknowledgements

Hello! You've come to the part of the book where I give my thanks to all the people who have made the book what it is. I'm going to thank my editor (spoiler for you right there), my agent and my manager etc., but I think the person who has made this book what it actually is, is you! You're the reader, the person the book was written for. Thank you for taking the time out of your busy life (MumLife or otherwise) to read this. I hope you've found it useful or entertaining or interesting in some way. I hope I haven't made you an emotional wreck! I'm a bit of a wreck after writing it, let me tell you!

A huge and heartfelt thank you must first go to my publishing team at Bonnier Books, for taking a leap of faith in me and letting me write a book so different from all my others. Beth Eynon, my non-fiction editor, you're the best! Thank you so much for letting me delve into all the hard topics as well as the fluffy ones. I know some of them have been challenging and emotional, but your constant kind support and cheerleading has meant the world to me. My agent Meghan and I love you. We want you to adopt us. (A real thing we've said.)

Big thank you also to my fiction editor Sarah Bauer, who has been such a support throughout *MumLife* and held off on chasing me for any other deadlines whilst I missed all the deadlines for this one, haha! Alex May in production; Ali Nazari and Stephen Dumughn in marketing; Francesca Russell and Karen Stretch in publicity; Stuart Finglass, Mark Williams, Vincent Kelleher in sales; Emily Rough in design and Alba Proko in audio – thank you for all your hard work, time and effort, you are so appreciated.

You may not know this, but this is the first book I've had help to draft and write. I spent hours and hours on the phone to Lucy Brazier, pouring my overemotional heart out about my mum, her death, the bad things that followed, the births of my babies and the good things that followed them. Lucy listened, typed notes, drafted up chapters and then I worked on those, making them mine, adding my voice, tweaking and twiddling and adding all the bits I'd forgotten. Lucy, you were far more than your role required. You helped me share things I'd never said out loud and now they are proudly in this book. Thank you so much for helping me, I'd have never been able to put pen to paper (or fingers to keyboard) without this initial support from you. I hope our paths cross again.

Thank you to my copy-editor Liz Marvin and proof-reader Jane Donovan – I'm sorry for all the spelling mistakes! Thank God for you two and your amazing, accurate eyes!!

Kate Parkin, the Bonnier Big Cheese MD, thank you for championing me and letting me write books with you. It's such an honour to be part of this team, I love coming into your London offices (the Maltesers at meetings are always a delightful bonus!) and I have loved all my years with you. I hope there are many more! Thank you for having me.

Those were my professional thank yous. Now for the others! Some of the people I'm thanking will feel really cringe about this because we're not the type to do any kind of feelings, haha.

To my management team at Gleam Futures, thanks guyyyyzz. You see!! It's hard to even type seriously! Abigail Bergstrom, there is no better literary agent than you! For all these years, you've been the best. Dom Smales, Gleam Big Cheese, thanks for keeping me on your books, even when I say inappropriate things at events and cry drunk on your wife's shoulder – you're good people!

Alrighty, Meghan Peterson, my manager, or (her official title) Meghan the Machine. You've advised, supported and cared throughout this process. Thank you for being there every step of the way, having hard chats about the hard bits, laughing with the good bits and your understanding of everything in between. You have been sound support and a long-suffering listener every day. Where would I be without you? Best you don't answer that, really.

The next bit of the book process is helping it find its way to your hands and my wonderful publicist, Charlotte Belle Tobin, will shine bright in this department, I know. She is the Queen of Publicity and deserves a big thank you, too!

Of course, my biggest thanks for a book about motherhood have to go to the people who made me a mother, my daughters Darcy and Pearl. Girls, I hope you read this when you are older! Maybe don't read the bits about mummy going on those awful dates, but just the bits where I talk about how much I love you or about your amazing granny in Heaven – she'd have loved you so much too.

I know this is a book about mums but I wanted to take a moment to thank my Dad. Some of this book will have been hard for him to read, a lot of it new information. He knew I was writing this and even when I asked if he minded me sharing so much, he was supportive, noting that it was my story to tell and I should be able to tell it however I want. That takes a lot of courage from a parent and I appreciate you for that, Dad. You've always encouraged me to do whatever I want, never held me back or dissuaded me from anything. Thank you for loving Mum, for removing me from a terrible situation in the sad years and for bringing Tina into our lives – how happy we all are now! Hurrah!

Final one before you all nod off with how long this is, thank you to all the mums in my life. All the women who have loved, guided and supported me. You've had my back when my own mum couldn't and I am forever grateful.

Dear reader, if you have a mum around, tell her she's special. If you're a mummy yourself, give those sweet babies a squeeze.

Big loves from me,
Louise xxxx

**If you loved *MumLife*,
you'll love Louise Pentland's novels . . .**

Robin Wilde is an awesome single mum. She's great at her job. Her best friend Lacey and bonkers Auntie Kath love her and little Lyla to the moon and back. From the outside, everything looks just fine.

But behind the mask she carefully applies every day, things sometimes feel . . . grey. And lonely.

So after four years (and two months and twenty-four days) of single-mum-dom, Robin Wilde has decided it's time to Change. Her. Life!

With a little courage, creativity and help from the wonderful women around her, Robin is about to embark on quite an adventure . . .

*Out now*

**Follow the story of Robin Wilde in the next two novels in the series:**

*Out now*

# JOIN MY READERS' CLUB

Thank you so much for reading my book!

If you enjoyed *MumLife*, why not join my Readers' Club*, Pentland Post, where I will tell you – before I tell anyone else – about my writing life and all the latest news about my books.

Visit www.LouisePentlandNovel.com to sign up!

Louise xxx

* Just so you know, your data is private and confidential and it will never be passed on to a third party. I'll only ever be in touch now and again about book news, and if you want to unsubscribe, you can do that at any time.